DOWN-HOME COOKIN'

HEARTY SOUPS, STEWS & BREADS

Potato & Cheddar Soup

2 cups water
2 cups red potatoes, peeled and cut into
  cubes
3 tablespoons butter or margarine
1 small onion, finely chopped
3 tablespoons all-purpose flour
  Red and black pepper to taste
3 cups milk
½ teaspoon sugar
1 cup shredded Cheddar cheese
1 cup cubed cooked ham

Bring water to a boil in large saucepan. Add
potatoes and cook until tender. Drain,
reserving liquid. Measure 1 cup, adding water
if necessary. Melt butter in saucepan over
medium heat. Add onion; cook and stir until
tender but not brown. Add flour; season with
red and black pepper. Cook 3 to 4 minutes.
Gradually add potatoes, reserved liquid, milk
and sugar to onion mixture; stir well. Add
cheese and ham. Simmer over low heat 30
minutes, stirring frequently.

Makes 12 servings

Turkey Split Pea Soup

Butterball® turkey carcass
2 cups cubed cooked
   BUTTERBALL® turkey
   (¾ pound)
Water
1 package (16 ounces) green
   split peas, washed
2 large carrots, sliced
1 cup chopped onion
2 cubes chicken bouillon
½ teaspoon salt
½ teaspoon ground black
   pepper
1 bay leaf

Place turkey carcass in Dutch
oven. Add 8 cups water. Bring to
boil over high heat; reduce heat to
low. Cover and simmer 1 hour.
Remove carcass. Strip turkey from
bones; reserve turkey. Discard
carcass. Strain broth. Measure
broth and add water to make 8
cups. Combine broth, turkey and
remaining ingredients in Dutch
oven. Bring mixture to boil over
high heat; reduce heat to low.
Cover and simmer 1 hour, stirring
occasionally.

Makes 8 servings (10 cups)

Sweet Potato Quick Bread

1¼ cups KELLOGG'S®
   ALL-BRAN® cereal,
   divided
¼ cup finely chopped pecans,
   divided
1 tablespoon all-purpose flour
1 tablespoon margarine
2 cups all-purpose flour
2 teaspoons baking powder
½ teaspoon baking soda
½ teaspoon salt (optional)
½ teaspoon cinnamon
½ teaspoon nutmeg
½ cup sugar
¼ cup margarine
2 eggs
1 cup low fat buttermilk
1 can (16 ounces) sweet
   potatoes, drained and
   mashed
Nonstick cooking spray

1. In small mixing bowl, combine
¼ cup Kellogg's® All-Bran® cereal,
2 tablespoons pecans and the 1
tablespoon flour. Cut in the 1
tablespoon margarine until
mixture resembles coarse crumbs.
Set aside for topping.

2. Stir together the 2 cups flour,
baking powder, baking soda, salt
cinnamon and nutmeg. Set aside.

3. In large mixing bowl, beat sugar
and ¼ cup margarine until light
and fluffy. Add eggs, buttermilk
and sweet potatoes; beat well. Add
dry ingredients, mixing only until
combined. Stir in remaining
Kellogg's® All-Bran® cereal.

4. Lightly coat 9×5-inch loaf pan
with cooking spray and sprinkle
with remaining 2 tablespoons
pecans. Pour batter into pan;
sprinkle with reserved cereal and
nut topping; press lightly.

Chunky Beef Chili

5. Bake at 350°F for 1 hour, 10 minutes or until toothpick inserted in center comes out clean. Cool 10 minutes; remove from pan. Let cool completely before slicing.

Makes 1 loaf, 15 slices

Chunky Beef Chili

2 tablespoons vegetable oil
2½ pounds boneless beef chuck, cut into ½-inch pieces
1 cup coarsely chopped onion
1 cup chopped green bell pepper
2 cloves garlic, minced
1 teaspoon salt
1 can (28 ounces) Italian-style plum tomatoes, broken up and undrained
1 cup water
1 can (6 ounces) tomato paste
3 tablespoons chili powder
1 teaspoon dried oregano leaves
¼ to ½ teaspoon crushed red pepper
1 can (15½ ounces) red kidney beans, drained
6 tablespoons shredded sharp Cheddar cheese
6 tablespoons chopped onion

Heat oil in large skillet or Dutch oven over medium-high heat. Add boneless beef chuck pieces, 1 cup chopped onion, green pepper and garlic; cook until beef is evenly browned. Pour off drippings. Sprinkle salt over beef. Add tomatoes, water, tomato paste, chili powder, oregano and crushed red pepper. Cover tightly; reduce heat and simmer 1½ hours or until beef is tender. Add beans; continue cooking, uncovered, 20 to 30 minutes. Serve with cheese and additional chopped onion.

Makes 8 servings

*Favorite recipe from **National Live Stock & Meat Board***

Apple Cheddar Muffins

 1 egg, slightly beaten
 ½ cup milk
 ¼ cup vegetable oil
 1 cup applesauce
 ¼ cup sugar
 1½ cups all-purpose flour
 2 teaspoons baking powder
 ½ teaspoon salt
 ½ teaspoon ground cinnamon
 ½ cup (2 ounces) SARGENTO®
    Classic Supreme®
    Shredded Mild or Sharp
    Cheddar Cheese

In large bowl, combine egg, milk, oil, applesauce and sugar. Sift flour, baking powder, salt and cinnamon together; add all at once with Cheddar cheese to egg mixture. Stir only until flour mixture is moistened (batter will be lumpy). Divide batter evenly among 12 greased muffin cups. (Cups will be more than ⅔ full.) Bake at 400°F for about 20 minutes or until wooden pick inserted in center comes out clean. Let cool in muffin pan 5 minutes. Run knife around outer edges of each muffin; turn out onto rack to cool completely.

Makes 12 muffins

Cheddar Chowder

 2 cups boiling water
 2 cups cauliflowerets
 1 cup diced potatoes
 ½ cup sliced carrots
 ½ cup sliced celery
 ¼ cup chopped onion
 1½ teaspoons salt
 ¼ teaspoon pepper
 ¼ cup butter or margarine
 ¼ cup flour
 2 cups milk
 2 cups (8 ounces)
    SARGENTO® Classic
    Supreme® or Fancy
    Supreme® Shredded Mild
    or Sharp Cheddar Cheese
 1 cup cubed cooked ham
    (optional)

In large saucepan, combine water, cauliflower, potatoes, carrots, celery, onion, salt and pepper. Bring to a boil over medium-high heat; cover and simmer 10 minutes. Do not drain. In large saucepan, melt butter. Stir in flour and milk; heat to boiling. Continue simmering, stirring constantly, until thickened. Add Cheddar cheese; stir until melted. Add undrained vegetable mixture and ham, if used. Heat through, but do not boil.

Makes about 8 servings

Left to right: Apple Cheddar Muffins; Cheddar Chowder

Flaky Southern Biscuits

2 cups all-purpose flour
1 tablespoon baking powder
½ teaspoon salt
½ cup chilled vegetable
shortening
¾ cup cold milk

Preheat oven to 425°F. In large
bowl, combine flour, baking
powder and salt. With pastry
blender or 2 knives, cut in
shortening until mixture resembles
coarse meal. Stir in milk just until
dough holds together. On lightly
floured board, knead gently about
1 minute. With floured rolling pin,
roll dough ½ inch thick. With
floured biscuit cutter, cut dough
into 2½- to 3-inch rounds. Place
1 inch apart on ungreased cookie
sheet. Bake 12 to 15 minutes or
until lightly browned. Serve hot.

Makes 10 biscuits

*Favorite recipe from **The McIlhenny
Company***

Bacon Brunch Buns

Bacon Brunch Buns

1 loaf (1 pound) frozen bread
dough
2 tablespoons (½ package)
HIDDEN VALLEY
RANCH® Original Ranch®
with Bacon salad
dressing mix
¼ cup unsalted butter or
margarine, melted
1 cup shredded Cheddar
cheese
2 egg yolks
½ tablespoons cold water
3 tablespoons sesame seeds

Thaw bread dough according to
package directions. Preheat oven
to 375°F. On floured board, roll
dough into rectangle about 18×7
inches. In small bowl, whisk
together salad dressing mix and
butter. Spread mixture on dough;
sprinkle with cheese. Roll up
tightly, jelly-roll style, pinching
seam to seal. Cut into 16 slices.

Place slices cut-side down on
greased jelly-roll pan. Cover with
plastic wrap and let rise until
doubled in bulk, about 1 hour. In
small bowl, beat egg yolks and
water; brush mixture over buns.
Sprinkle with sesame seeds. Bake
until golden brown, 25 to 30
minutes. Serve warm.

Makes 16 buns

Creamy Shell Soup

4 cups water
3 to 4 chicken pieces
1 cup diced onions
¼ cup chopped celery
¼ cup minced parsley or 1
    tablespoon dried parsley
    flakes
1 bay leaf
1 teaspoon salt
¼ teaspoon white pepper
2 medium potatoes, diced
4 to 5 green onions, chopped
3 chicken bouillon cubes
½ teaspoon seasoned salt
½ teaspoon poultry seasoning
4 cups milk
2 cups medium shell macaroni,
    cooked and drained
¼ cup butter or margarine
¼ cup all-purpose flour
    Ground nutmeg
    Chopped fresh parsley

Simmer water, chicken, diced onions, celery, minced parsley, bay leaf, salt and pepper in Dutch oven until chicken is tender. Remove bay leaf; discard. Remove chicken; cool. Skin, debone and cut into small cubes; set aside.

Add potatoes, green onions, bouillon cubes, seasoned salt and poultry seasoning to broth. Simmer 15 minutes. Add milk, macaroni and chicken; return to simmer.

Melt butter in skillet over medium heat. Add flour, stirring constantly, until mixture begins to brown. Add to soup; blend well. Let soup simmer on very low heat 20 minutes to blend flavors. Season to taste. Garnish with nutmeg and chopped parsley.

Makes 8 servings

Favorite recipe from North Dakota Wheat Commission

Orange Pecan Bread

1¾ cups all-purpose flour
¾ cup sugar
1 teaspoon baking powder
½ teaspoon baking soda
½ teaspoon salt
¾ cup Florida orange juice
1 egg, lightly beaten
2 tablespoons butter or
    margarine, melted and
    cooled
1 tablespoon grated fresh
    orange peel
½ teaspoon almond extract
½ cup chopped pitted dates
½ cup chopped pecans

Preheat oven to 350°F.

In large bowl, combine flour, sugar, baking powder, baking soda and salt. In separate bowl, combine orange juice, egg, butter, orange peel and almond extract.

Make a well in center of flour mixture and pour in orange juice mixture; stir until just combined. Stir in dates and pecans.

Pour batter into greased 9×5×3-inch loaf pan. Bake at 350°F for 50 minutes or until wooden pick inserted in center comes out clean Cool in pan 10 minutes. Remove from pan. Cool completely on wire rack.   *Makes 1 loaf*

Favorite recipe from Florida Department of Citrus

Creamy Shell Soup

Classic Banana Bread

2 extra-ripe, medium DOLE®
   Bananas, peeled
¾ cup brown sugar, packed
½ cup margarine, softened
1 egg
¼ cup dairy sour cream
1 teaspoon vanilla extract
2¼ cups all-purpose flour
1 teaspoon baking powder
½ teaspoon baking soda
½ teaspoon salt
½ teaspoon ground cinnamon
1 cup DOLE® Chopped
   Almonds

• Preheat oven to 350°F.

• Process bananas in blender;
measure 1 cup.

• Beat sugar and margarine until
light and fluffy. Beat in egg. Beat
in processed bananas, sour cream
and vanilla until blended.

• Combine flour, baking powder,
baking soda, salt and cinnamon.
Stir into banana mixture. Stir in
almonds.

• Pour into greased 9×5-inch loaf
pan. Bake in preheated oven 65 to
70 minutes or until wooden pick
inserted in center comes out clean.
Cool in pan 10 minutes. Invert
onto wire rack to cool completely.
Makes 1 loaf

Top to bottom: Classic Bana
Bread; Poppy Seed Bread

Poppy Seed Bread

1 cup sugar
½ cup margarine, softened
2 eggs
1 teaspoon grated lemon peel
2 extra-ripe, medium DOLE®
   Bananas
2 cups all-purpose flour
2 teaspoons baking powder
½ teaspoon salt
¼ teaspoon ground cinnamon
¼ cup poppy seeds

• Preheat oven to 350°F.

• In large bowl, beat sugar and margarine until light and fluffy. Beat in eggs and lemon peel. Process bananas in blender; measure 1 cup.

• In small bowl, combine flour, baking powder, salt and cinnamon. Add flour mixture to egg mixture alternately with processed bananas, ending with flour mixture. Stir in poppy seeds. Spoon into greased 9×5-inch loaf pan.

Bake in preheated oven 60 to 70 minutes until wooden pick inserted in center comes out clean. Cool slightly in pan. Invert onto wire rack to cool completely.

Makes 1 loaf

Hearty Chicken Noodle Soup

1 can (49½ ounces) chicken broth
1 cup water
1 cup sliced carrots
½ cup chopped celery
¼ cup chopped onion
⅛ teaspoon white pepper
1 recipe ALL-BRAN®
  Noodles (recipe follows)
2 cups chopped, cooked chicken
2 tablespoons chopped parsley

. In 4-quart saucepan, combine broth, water, carrots, celery, onion and pepper. Cook over medium heat until mixture boils. Reduce heat; cover and simmer 5 minutes.

2. Add All-Bran® Noodles and return mixture to a boil. Simmer 10 minutes or until noodles are tender, stirring occasionally. Stir in chicken and continue to cook 1 minute longer. Remove from heat; stir in parsley. Serve hot.
Makes 6 servings (1½ cups each)

All-Bran® Noodles

1 cup KELLOGG'S®
  ALL-BRAN® cereal,
  crushed into fine crumbs
½ cup whole wheat flour
½ cup all-purpose flour
½ teaspoon salt
¼ cup skim milk
2 egg whites
6 cups water or chicken broth

1. In large bowl, combine Kellogg's® All-Bran® cereal, whole wheat flour, all-purpose flour and salt. Mix in milk and egg whites adding enough extra flour to make a stiff dough, if necessary.

2. Roll dough on well-floured surface to ¹⁄₁₆-inch thickness. Let dry 1 hour. Cut dough into 3-inch strips. Flour dough slightly, if necessary. Layer 4 to 5 strips on top of each other. Cut each stack crosswise into ¼-inch noodles.

3. Spread noodles loosely on floured surface; let dry about 2 hours.
Makes 6 servings (½ cup each)

Savory Apple Bread

- 1 tablespoon butter or margarine
- 1 Golden Delicious apple, peeled, cored and diced
- ½ cup chopped onion
- 1 (16-ounce) package hot roll mix
- 1 cup shredded Cheddar cheese
- 2 tablespoons chopped sweet red pepper
- 1 tablespoon caraway seeds
- 1 cup hot (not boiling) water
- 1 egg, beaten

In small skillet, heat butter. Add apple and onion; cook and stir until both are tender. Set aside. In large bowl, combine hot roll mix, cheese, red pepper and caraway seeds. Stir in water, egg and reserved apple mixture; stir until dough pulls away from side of bowl.

Turn dough out onto lightly floured surface; knead 5 minutes. Cover dough with mixing bowl and let rest 5 minutes.

Grease 1½-quart round baking dish; place dough in dish. Score an "X" on top of dough with sharp knife. Cover dough and let rise 30 minutes.

When dough has risen, heat oven to 375°F; bake bread 35 minutes or until golden and hollow-sounding when gently tapped. Cool on wire rack.

Makes 8 servings

*Favorite recipe from **Washington Apple Commission***

Savory Apple Bread

Corn and Potato Chowder

Nonstick cooking spray
1 cup chopped onions
½ cup sliced green pepper
½ cup sliced red pepper
1 large clove garlic, minced
2 cans (10½ ounces *each*)
    lower salt chicken broth
1 can (16½ ounces)
    no-salt-added cream style
    corn
1 can (15¼ ounces)
    no-salt-added whole kernel
    corn, drained
1 can (16 ounces) whole
    potatoes, drained, sliced
¼ teaspoon ground cumin
4 dashes red pepper sauce
¼ to ½ teaspoon black pepper
2 slices bacon, fried crisp,
    drained, crumbled
Minced parsley

Spray large saucepan with cooking spray; cook and stir onions, peppers and garlic until tender. Stir in chicken broth, corn, potatoes and cumin; heat to boiling. Reduce heat and simmer, uncovered, 15 to 20 minutes. Stir in red pepper sauce and pepper. Spoon into bowls; sprinkle with bacon and parsley.

Makes 4 servings
(about 2 cups each)

Favorite recipe from Canned Food Information Council

Bayou Jambalaya

Bayou Jambalaya

1 medium onion, sliced
½ cup chopped green bell
    pepper
1 clove garlic, minced
1 cup uncooked white rice
2 tablespoons vegetable oil
1 cup water
¾ cup HEINZ® Tomato
    Ketchup
1 tablespoon HEINZ® Vinegar
⅛ teaspoon black pepper
⅛ teaspoon ground red pepper
1 cup cubed cooked ham
1 medium tomato, coarsely
    chopped
½ pound raw medium shrimp,
    shelled, deveined

In large skillet, cook and stir onion, green pepper, garlic and rice in oil until onion is tender. Stir in water, ketchup, vinegar, black pepper, red pepper, ham and tomato. Cover; simmer 20 to 25 minutes or until rice is tender. Add shrimp; simmer, uncovered, 3 to 5 minutes or until shrimp turn pink, stirring occasionally.

Makes 4 to 6 servings
(about 6 cups)

Navajo Lamb Stew with Cornmeal Dumplings

2 pounds lean lamb stew meat
    with bones, cut into 2-inch
    pieces *or* 1½ pounds lean
    boneless lamb, cut into
    1½-inch cubes
1 teaspoon salt
½ teaspoon pepper
2½ tablespoons vegetable oil,
    divided
1 large onion, chopped
1 clove garlic, minced
4 cups water
2 tablespoons tomato paste
2 teaspoons chili powder
1 teaspoon ground coriander
3 small potatoes, cut into
    1½-inch chunks
2 large carrots, cut into 1-inch
    pieces
1 package (10 ounces) frozen
    whole kernel corn
⅓ cup coarsely chopped celery
    leaves
    Cornmeal Dumplings (recipe
    follows)
    Whole celery leaves for
    garnish

Sprinkle meat with salt and
pepper. Heat 2 tablespoons oil in
5-quart Dutch oven over medium-
high heat. Add meat a few pieces
at a time; cook until browned.
Transfer meat to medium bowl.
Heat remaining ½ tablespoon oil
over medium heat. Add onion and
garlic; cook until onion is tender.
Stir in water, tomato paste, chili
powder and coriander. Return
meat to Dutch oven. Add potatoes,
carrots, corn and chopped celery
leaves. Bring to a boil. Cover;
reduce heat and simmer 1 hour
and 15 minutes or until meat is
tender. During last 15 minutes of
cooking, prepare Cornmeal
Dumplings. Drop dough onto stew
to make 6 dumplings. Cover and
simmer 18 minutes or until
dumplings are firm to the touch
and wooden pick inserted in
center comes out clean. To serve,
spoon stew onto individual plates;
serve with dumplings. Garnish with
whole celery leaves.

Makes 6 servings

Cornmeal Dumplings
½ cup yellow cornmeal
½ cup all-purpose flour
1 teaspoon baking powder
¼ teaspoon salt
2½ tablespoons cold butter or
    margarine
½ cup milk

Combine cornmeal, flour, baking
powder and salt in medium bowl.
Cut in butter with fingers, pastry
blender or 2 knives until mixture
resembles coarse crumbs. Make a
well in center; pour in milk all at
once and stir with fork until
mixture forms dough.

*Navajo Lamb Stew with
Cornmeal Dumplings*

Preheat oven to 350°F. In small bowl, combine nuts, brown sugar and nutmeg; set aside. Stir together flour, baking powder and baking soda; set aside. In large mixer bowl, beat granulated sugar and margarine until fluffy. Add eggs, 1 at a time, beating well after each addition. Gradually beat in ReaLemon® brand. Add milk alternately with flour mixture; stir well. Spoon half of batter into greased and floured 9×5-inch loaf pan. Sprinkle half of nut mixture over batter; top with remaining batter, spreading to pan edge. Top with remaining nut mixture. Bake 50 to 55 minutes or until wooden pick inserted near center comes out clean. Cool 15 minutes; remove from pan. Cool completely. Store tightly wrapped.

Makes one 9×5-inch loaf

Streusel Lemon Bread

Streusel Lemon Bread

½ cup finely chopped nuts
¼ cup firmly packed light brown sugar
½ teaspoon ground nutmeg
2 cups unsifted flour
1 teaspoon baking powder
½ teaspoon baking soda
1¼ cups granulated sugar
½ cup margarine or butter, softened
3 eggs
½ cup REALEMON® Lemon Juice from Concentrate
½ cup BORDEN® or MEADOW GOLD® Milk

Old-Fashioned Carrot Soup

1 (46-fluid ounce) can COLLEGE INN® Chicken Broth
1½ pounds carrots, cut in 1-inch pieces
4 large onions, coarsely chopped
3 stalks celery, cut in 1-inch pieces
¼ cup chopped parsley
¼ cup BLUE BONNET® 75% Vegetable Oil Spread
¼ cup all-purpose flour
2 cups milk*

* For thinner soup, add additional milk until desired consistency.

In large heavy pot, over medium-high heat, bring broth, carrots, onions, celery and parsley to a boil. Cover; reduce heat and simmer until vegetables are tender, about 30 minutes. Cool slightly. In blender container or food processor, blend mixture in batches until smooth; set aside.

In same saucepan, melt spread; blend in flour. Stir in carrot mixture and milk. Cook, stirring occasionally, until heated through. Garnish with additional parsley, if desired.   *Makes 8 servings*

Cider Stew

2 pounds stew beef, cut into
    1-inch cubes
2 tablespoons BLUE BONNET®
    75% Vegetable Oil Spread
¼ cup all-purpose flour
2 cups water
1 cup apple cider
½ cup A.1.® Steak Sauce
2 teaspoons dried thyme leaves
½ teaspoon ground black
    pepper
1 bay leaf
3 medium potatoes, peeled and
    cut into 1-inch cubes
3 medium carrots, sliced
1 medium onion, chopped
1 (10-ounce) package frozen
    cut green beans

In large heavy pot, over medium-high heat, brown half the beef at a time in spread. Return beef to pot. Stir in flour. Gradually stir in water, cider and steak sauce. Over high heat, bring to a boil; stir in thyme, pepper and bay leaf.

Reduce heat to low; cover and simmer for 2 hours.

Add potatoes, carrots, onion and beans. Cover and cook for 30 minutes more or until vegetables are tender. Discard bay leaf before serving.   *Makes 6 to 8 servings*

Golden Hearty Cornbread

1¼ cups cornmeal
½ cup all-purpose flour
½ teaspoon baking soda
⅛ teaspoon salt (optional)
½ cup KELLOGG'S®
    ALL-BRAN® cereal
¾ cup skim milk
2 egg whites, slightly beaten
3 tablespoons vegetable oil
1 cup no-salt-added whole
    kernel corn, drained
½ cup reduced fat Cheddar
    cheese
½ cup chopped green onions
    Nonstick cooking spray

1. Stir together cornmeal, flour, baking soda and salt. Set aside.

2. In large mixing bowl, combine Kellogg's® All-Bran® cereal and milk. Let stand 2 minutes or until cereal is slightly softened. Add egg whites, oil, corn, cheese and green onions. Add flour mixture, stirring just until combined. Spread batter into 8×8×2-inch baking pan coated with cooking spray.

3. Bake at 400°F about 40 minutes or until golden brown. Serve warm.
     Makes 9 servings

HARVEST VEGETABLE DISHES

Fresh Vegetable Casserole

8 small new potatoes
8 baby carrots
1 small cauliflower, broken into florets
4 stalks asparagus, cut into 1-inch pieces
3 tablespoons butter or margarine
3 tablespoons all-purpose flour
2 cups milk
  Salt
  Pepper
¾ cup (3 ounces) shredded Cheddar
    cheese
  Chopped fresh cilantro

Cook vegetables until crisp-tender. Arrange
vegetables in buttered 2-quart casserole. To
make sauce, melt butter in medium saucepan
over medium heat. Stir in flour until smooth.
Gradually stir in milk. Cook until thickened,
stirring constantly. Season to taste with salt
and pepper. Add cheese, stirring until cheese
is melted. Pour sauce over vegetables and
sprinkle with cilantro. Bake in preheated
350°F oven 15 minutes or until heated
through.   *Makes 4 to 6 servings*

Scalloped Onion & Almond Casserole

1 pound pearl onions
¼ cup unsalted butter or
    margarine
4 celery stalks, chopped
    (1½ cups)
5 green onions chopped
    (1 cup)
5 tablespoons all-purpose flour
1 teaspoon salt
1 teaspoon TABASCO® pepper
    sauce
½ teaspoon freshly ground
    pepper
2 cups half-and-half
⅔ cup sliced, blanched almonds
½ cup grated Parmesan cheese
    (1½ ounces)
    Toasted sliced almonds, if
    desired
    Celery leaves, if desired

Lightly butter 1½-quart casserole.
Using sharp knife, remove root end
from each onion; set onions aside.
Fill 4- to 6-quart saucepan half full
of water; bring to a boil over
medium-high heat. Add onions;
parboil 1 minute. Drain in
colander; run under water to cool.
When onions are cool enough to
handle, peel by grasping between
your thumb and forefinger at stem
end and squeezing lightly. The
peel should slip off easily. Set
peeled onions aside. In a heavy
12-inch skillet over medium heat,
melt butter. Add celery; cook 5
minutes. Add peeled onions and
green onions; stir to blend.
Sprinkle flour into skillet; stir 3 to
4 minutes.

Blend in salt, TABASCO sauce and
pepper. Slowly stir in half-and-half.
Cook about 5 minutes; fold in ⅔
cup blanched almonds and grated
cheese. Pour into prepared
casserole. Bake in a preheated
350°F oven until bubbly and
lightly browned, 25 minutes. Top
with toasted almonds and celery
leaves, if desired.
    Makes 4 to 6 servings

Quick Dills

6 pounds 3- to 5-inch pickling
    cucumbers
6 cups water
3 cups white vinegar (labeled
    5% acidity)
½ cup KERR® Pickling Salt
12 to 24 heads fresh dill
6 to 12 cloves garlic (optional)

Wash cucumbers and remove
1/16-inch from blossom end. Soak in
ice water for 24 hours. Drain.
Combine water, vinegar and
pickling salt in 6-quart saucepan.
Bring to a boil over high heat.
Meanwhile, place 1 to 2 heads of
dill and 1 to 2 cloves garlic in hot
quart jars. Firmly pack cucumbers
into jars, leaving ½-inch
headspace. Top with additional 1
to 2 heads of dill. Immediately fill
jars with hot vinegar mixture,
leaving ½-inch headspace.
Carefully run nonmetal spatula
down inside of jars to remove
trapped air bubbles. Wipe jar tops
and threads clean. Place lids on
hot jars and screw bands on firmly.
Process in Boiling Water Canner
(page 29) for 15 minutes. For best
flavor, let stand 2 to 3 weeks in
jars before serving.
    Makes 6 quarts

Okra-Bacon Casserole

1½ pounds young fresh okra
3 large tomatoes, chopped
1 medium onion, chopped
1 small green pepper, chopped
½ teaspoon TABASCO® pepper
    sauce, divided
5 slices bacon

Preheat oven to 350°F. Slice okra
into thin rounds. In greased
2½-quart casserole, arrange okra,
tomatoes, onion and green pepper.
Season with TABASCO sauce.
Place bacon on top. Bake
uncovered 1½ hours or until okra
is tender.   *Makes 6 to 8 servings*

Note: Two (10-ounce) packages
frozen okra, thawed, may be
substituted for fresh okra. Bake
casserole 1 hour.

Old-Fashioned Cole Slaw

½ cup reduced calorie
    mayonnaise
2 tablespoons milk
1 tablespoon white vinegar
½ teaspoon sugar
    Salt and pepper to taste
1 bag (1 pound) DOLE® Cole
    Slaw Blend

Combine mayonnaise, milk,
vinegar, sugar, salt and pepper in
glass measure.

Place Cole Slaw Blend in large
bowl. Pour dressing over mixture.
Toss to coat with dressing.

Cover; refrigerate at least 1 hour
for flavors to blend.
        Makes 8 servings

Country Style Potatoes Au Gratin

2 tablespoons BLUE BONNET®
    75% Vegetable Oil Spread
2 tablespoons all-purpose flour
1½ cups milk
1 cup grated Swiss cheese
½ cup GREY POUPON®
    Parisian Spicy Brown
    Mustard
2 pounds medium potatoes,
    thinly sliced
1 medium green pepper, cut
    into strips
1 medium onion, sliced

In medium saucepan, melt spread;
blend in flour. Slowly stir in milk;
cook until mixture thickens and
begins to boil. Remove from heat;
blend in cheese and mustard.

In 2-quart shallow baking dish,
arrange half the potatoes, pepper
and onion; top with half the
cheese sauce. Repeat layers. Cover
and bake at 375°F for 50 minutes.
Remove cover. *Increase oven
temperature to 400°F and bake 20
minutes more or until potatoes are
tender.*   *Makes 8 servings*

Corn Pudding Soufflé

2 tablespoons butter or
    margarine
2 tablespoons all-purpose flour
    Half-and-half
1 can (17 ounces) whole
    kernel corn, drained,
    liquid reserved
¼ cup canned chopped green
    chilies, drained
    Dash garlic powder
2 eggs, separated
¼ cup cream-style cottage
    cheese

Melt butter in medium saucepan
over medium heat. Stir in flour
until smooth. Add enough
half-and-half to corn liquid to
measure 1 cup. Gradually stir
liquid into saucepan. Continue
stirring until sauce is smooth and
hot. Stir in corn, chilies and garlic
powder.

Bring to a boil over medium heat,
stirring constantly. Reduce heat to
low. Beat egg yolks in small bowl.
Stir about ¼ cup of the hot sauce
into egg yolks, beating constantly.
Stir egg yolk mixture back into
sauce. Remove from heat; stir in
cottage cheese. Beat egg whites in
narrow bowl until stiff peaks form.
Fold egg whites into corn mixture.
Pour into ungreased 1½-quart
soufflé dish. Bake in preheated
350°F oven 30 minutes or until
wooden pick inserted in center
comes out clean.

Makes 4 to 6 servings

Creamy Baked Mashed Potatoes

1 envelope LIPTON® Recipe
    Secrets™ Vegetable
    Soup Mix
4 cups hot mashed potatoes*
1 cup shredded Cheddar or
    Swiss cheese (about
    4 ounces)
½ cup chopped green onions
    (optional)
1 egg, slightly beaten
⅛ teaspoon LAWRY'S®
    Seasoned Pepper

MICROWAVE DIRECTIONS: In
lightly greased 1½-quart
microwavable casserole,
thoroughly combine all ingredients
except ¼ cup cheese. Microwave,
covered, at HIGH (100% power),
turning casserole occasionally, 7
minutes or until heated through.
Top with remaining cheese, then
let stand covered 5 minutes.

Makes about 8 servings

* Do not use salt when preparing
hot mashed potatoes.

CONVENTIONAL DIRECTIONS:
Preheat oven to 375°F. In lightly
greased 1½-quart casserole,
thoroughly combine all ingredients
except ¼ cup cheese. Bake 40
minutes. Top with remaining
cheese and bake an additional 5
minutes or until cheese is melted.

Corn Pudding Soufflé

Rosemary Garlic Potatoes

4 large red skin potatoes, cut
    into wedges (about
    2 pounds)
1½ teaspoons dried rosemary
    leaves
1 teaspoon garlic powder
2 tablespoons
    FLEISCHMANN'S®
    Margarine, melted

In large bowl, toss potatoes with
rosemary and garlic. On lightly
greased baking pan, arrange
potatoes in single layer; drizzle
with margarine. Broil 4 inches
from heat source for 25 to 30
minutes or until tender, turning
potatoes over once.

Makes 4 servings

Carrots Saucily Spiced

Carrots Saucily Spiced

1 pound carrots, cut into
    ½-inch diagonal slices
¼ cup HEINZ® Tomato
    Ketchup
1½ tablespoons light brown
    sugar
1 tablespoon butter or
    margarine
⅛ teaspoon ground allspice

In medium saucepan, cook carrots
in boiling water to cover until
crisp-tender; drain. In medium
skillet or saucepan, combine
ketchup, brown sugar, butter and
allspice; heat through. Add carrots;
turn and baste with sauce until
heated through.

Makes 4 to 6 servings
(about 2½ cups)

Red Cabbage 'n' Apples

¼ cup margarine or butter
⅓ cup REALEMON® Lemon
    Juice from Concentrate
¼ cup firmly packed light
    brown sugar
¼ cup water
½ teaspoon caraway seeds
½ teaspoon salt
4 cups shredded red cabbage
2 medium all-purpose apples,
    cored and coarsely
    chopped

In large saucepan, melt margarine;
stir in ReaLemon® brand, sugar,
water, caraway and salt. Add
cabbage and apples; bring to a
boil. Reduce heat; cover and
simmer 25 to 30 minutes.

Makes 6 to 8 servings

Acorn Squash with Maple Butter

2 medium acorn squash*
  LAWRY'S® Seasoned Salt
3 tablespoons IMPERIAL®
  Margarine or butter
3 tablespoons MRS.
  BUTTERWORTH'S® Maple
  Syrup
¼ teaspoon ground nutmeg
  (optional)

Pierce squash with fork. Bake in 375°F oven 1 to 1½ hours or until fork-tender. Cut squash in half crosswise. Slice off ends, if necessary, so halves will be level. Remove seeds. Sprinkle squash with Seasoned Salt. In baking dish, place squash cut-side up. Divide margarine and syrup among halves. Bake 5 minutes. Sprinkle with Seasoned Salt and nutmeg.

Makes 4 servings

* Butternut squash can be substituted for acorn squash.

Presentation: Serve in quarters or sliced ½ inch thick.

MICROWAVE DIRECTIONS:
Pierce squash in several places; microwave whole squash on HIGH (100% power) 10 to 12 minutes or until fork-tender; let stand 2 minutes and cut in half crosswise. Slice off ends, if necessary, so halves will be level. Remove seeds. Sprinkle squash with Seasoned Salt. In 13×9×2-inch microwavable baking dish, place squash cut-side up. Divide margarine and maple syrup among halves. Cover with plastic wrap, venting one corner. Microwave on HIGH (100% power) 30 seconds; brush syrup mixture over cut surface and microwave on HIGH (100% power) 30 seconds longer. Sprinkle with Seasoned Salt and nutmeg; let squash stand 3 minutes before serving.

Acorn Squash with Maple Butter

Green Beans with Pine Nuts

1 pound green beans, ends
    removed
2 tablespoons butter or
    margarine
2 tablespoons pine nuts
    Salt
    Pepper

Cook beans in 1 inch water in
covered 3-quart saucepan 4 to 8
minutes or until crisp-tender;
drain. Melt butter in large skillet
over medium heat. Add pine nuts;
cook, stirring frequently, until
golden. Add beans; stir gently to
coat beans with butter. Season
with salt and pepper to taste.

Makes 4 servings

Fresh Corn with Adobe Butter

½ teaspoon chili powder
1 teaspoon lime juice
¼ cup butter or margarine,
    softened
    Salt
4 ears yellow or white corn,
    husks and silk removed

Moisten chili powder with lime
juice in small bowl. Add butter;
stir until well blended. Season with
salt to taste. Place in small crock
or bowl. Place corn in 5-quart pan;
cover with cold water. Cover; bring
to a boil. Boil 1 minute. Turn off
heat; let stand 2 minutes or until
corn is tender. Drain. Serve with
butter mixture.

Makes 4 servings

Glazed Sweet Potatoes and Turnips

4 medium sweet potatoes,
    peeled, cut in chunks
4 medium turnips, peeled, cut
    in chunks
1 cup Florida orange juice
⅓ cup brown sugar
¼ cup butter or margarine,
    melted
½ teaspoon mace
½ teaspoon salt
2 Florida oranges, peeled,
    sliced

In large saucepan in 1-inch boiling
water, cook potatoes and turnips
until crisp-tender, about 30
minutes.

Preheat oven to 400°F.

Place vegetables in 2-quart shallow
baking dish. In small bowl
combine orange juice, sugar,
butter, mace and salt. Pour over
vegetables.

Bake, uncovered, in 400°F oven
about 30 minutes. Baste often with
pan juices. Vegetables are done
when pan juices are reduced and
vegetables are glazed.

Garnish with orange slices.

Makes 8 servings

*Favorite recipe from Florida
Department of Citrus*

*Top to bottom: Green Beans
with Pine Nuts; Fresh Corn
with Adobe Butter*

Tomato Ginger Apple Salad

2 Golden Delicious or Granny Smith apples, cored and sliced into ¼-inch rings
4 medium tomatoes, sliced into ¼-inch rings
¼ cup thinly sliced radishes
¼ cup chopped parsley
¼ cup vegetable oil
2 teaspoons grated fresh ginger
1 teaspoon sugar
1 teaspoon lemon juice
½ teaspoon grated lemon peel
Salt and pepper to taste
Parsley or cilantro sprigs (optional)

Tomato Ginger Apple Salad

Arrange apple and tomato slices alternately on serving platter; sprinkle with radishes and parsley. In small bowl, combine oil, ginger, sugar, lemon juice and lemon peel; season to taste with salt and pepper. Drizzle mixture over arranged salad. Marinate salad in refrigerator 1 to 2 hours. Garnish with parsley or cilantro sprigs, if desired.   *Makes 4 servings*

Favorite recipe from Washington Apple Commission

Country-Style Potato Salad

2 pounds cooked red potatoes, peeled and diced
3 green onions, cut into ½-inch pieces
10 cherry tomatoes, halved
2 hard-cooked eggs, chopped
⅓ cup mayonnaise
⅓ cup GREY POUPON® Dijon or Country Dijon Mustard
2 tablespoons red wine vinegar
½ teaspoon garlic powder
⅛ teaspoon ground black pepper

In large bowl, combine potatoes, green onions, tomatoes and eggs; set aside.

In small bowl, blend remaining ingredients; stir into potato mixture, tossing to coat well. Cover; chill at least 2 hours to blend flavors.

Makes 6 (1¼ cup) servings

Corn Relish

16 to 20 medium-size ears fresh
    corn in husks (about 10
    cups fresh whole kernel
    corn)
1½ cups chopped green bell
    peppers
1½ cups chopped red bell
    peppers
  1 cup chopped celery
  1 cup chopped onions
  4 cups white vinegar (labeled
    5% acidity)
2¼ cups sugar
  1 cup water
  2 tablespoons mustard seed
  1 tablespoon *plus* 1 teaspoon
    KERR® Pickling Salt
  1 teaspoon celery seed
  ½ teaspoon ground turmeric

Husk corn; remove silk and wash.
Drop in boiling water. Return to a
boil; boil 5 minutes. Immediately
dip in cold water. Cut kernels from
cobs. (Do not scrape cobs.)
Measure 10 cups cut corn.
Combine corn, peppers, celery,
onions, vinegar, sugar, water,
mustard seed, pickling salt, celery
seed and turmeric in 8-quart
saucepan. Bring to a boil over
medium-high heat; boil 15
minutes, stirring occasionally.

Immediately fill hot pint jars with
corn mixture, leaving ½-inch
headspace. Carefully run nonmetal
spatula down inside of jars to
remove trapped air bubbles. Wipe
jar tops and threads clean. Place
hot lids on jars; screw bands on
firmly. Process in Boiling Water
Canner (directions follow) 15
minutes.   *Makes 6 to 7 pints*

**Boiling Water Canner
Directions:** Examine jar tops. Tops
with defects will prevent jar from
sealing. Wash jars and keep hot to
prevent breakage when filled with
hot food and placed in canner for
processing. Jars to be processed in
Boiling Water Canner for less than
10 minutes need to be sterilized.
To sterilize, cover jars with water;
boil for 10 minutes. Leave in hot
water until ready to use.

Examine screwbands. Use only
those free from rust and dents.
Examine lids. Use only those free
from dents and scratches, with a
complete ring of sealing compound
in the groove. Wash lids; pour
boiling water over lids and leave
them in hot water for at least 3
minutes or until ready to use. Do
not boil or reuse lids.

Fill hot jars as directed, leaving
appropriate headspace. Prepare
only enough jars of food at one
time to fill canner. Place hot lids
on jars with sealing compound
next to jar top. Center on jars.
Screw bands on firmly.

Partially fill canner with water;
bring to a simmer. Using jar lifter,
place jars, without tipping, onto
rack in canner. Increase heat to
high; bring to a boil. Cover; reduce
heat slightly to maintain gentle,
steady boil. Begin timing. Be sure
water stays boiling and that it
covers jars by 2 inches, adding
more boiling water if needed.

When proper time is reached, turn
off heat. Remove jars with jar
lifter, making sure food does not
touch lid. Place on rack or dry
towel at least 1 inch apart, free
from drafts. Cool overnight. Do not
cover while cooling. Do not
retighten screwbands after
processing.

- Cut potatoes lengthwise into wedges. Brush with salad dressing. Season with onion salt and pepper.

- Place on greased 15×10×1-inch jelly roll pan.

- Bake at 375°F, 50 minutes or until tender and golden brown.

- Prepare Parma Dip and Hearty Barbecue Dip. Serve with potatoes.
  Makes 4 servings

Parma Dip
   1 cup MIRACLE WHIP® Light Reduced Calorie Salad Dressing
   ¼ cup (1 ounce) KRAFT® 100% Grated Parmesan Cheese
   ¼ cup milk
   1 tablespoon chopped chives

- Combine ingredients; mix well.
  Makes 1¼ cups

Hearty Barbecue Dip
   ½ cup MIRACLE WHIP® Light Reduced Calorie Salad Dressing
   ¼ cup KRAFT® Thick 'n Spicy Barbecue Sauce with Honey
   2 tablespoons chopped onion
   2 tablespoons chopped green pepper

- Combine ingredients; mix well.
  Makes 1 cup

Preparation time: 10 minutes
Baking time: 50 minutes
Tip: For a more blended flavor, prepare dips ahead of time. Cover; chill.

Baked Potato Spears

Baked Potato Spears

   3 large baking potatoes
   ¼ cup MIRACLE WHIP® Light Reduced Calorie Salad Dressing
   Onion salt
   Pepper
   Parma Dip (recipe follows)
   Hearty Barbecue Dip (recipe follows)

Creamy Corn Au Gratin

½ cup green onion slices
½ cup chopped red pepper
¼ cup PARKAY® Margarine,
    divided
2 (10-ounce) packages sweet
    corn, thawed, drained
½ pound VELVEETA®
    Pasteurized Process
    Cheese Spread, cubed
⅔ cup crushed tortilla chips
½ teaspoon Mexican seasoning
2 tablespoons chopped cilantro

• Cook and stir onions and pepper in 2 tablespoons margarine. Reduce heat to low.

• Stir in corn and process cheese spread. Cook 5 to 7 minutes or until process cheese spread is melted and mixture is thoroughly heated, stirring occasionally.

• Melt remaining margarine in separate pan; stir in tortilla chips and seasoning. Cook over medium heat 3 minutes; stir in cilantro.

• Spoon corn mixture into serving bowl; sprinkle with tortilla mixture. Garnish with additional cilantro and red pepper.
                    Makes 6 servings
Preparation time: 25 minutes

MICROWAVE DIRECTIONS:
Microwave onions, peppers and 2 tablespoons margarine in 1½-quart microwavable bowl on HIGH 2 to 3 minutes or until vegetables are tender. Stir in corn and process cheese spread. Microwave 5 to 7 minutes or until process cheese spread is melted and mixture is thoroughly heated, stirring every 3 minutes. Microwave remaining margarine in 1-quart microwavable bowl 1 minute. Stir in tortilla chips and seasoning. Microwave 2 minutes, stirring after 1 minute; stir in cilantro. Continue as directed.

Microwave Cooking time:
13 minutes

Variation: Substitute ¼ teaspoon ground cumin and ¼ teaspoon chili powder for Mexican seasoning.

Creamy Corn Au Gratin

HOMESTYLE SUPPERS

Texas-Style Beef Brisket

6 to 8 pounds boneless beef brisket
¾ cup finely chopped onion
2 teaspoons paprika
½ teaspoon freshly ground pepper
   Water
1 cup prepared steak sauce
   Special Sauce (recipe page 34)

Trim fat covering on brisket to ¼ inch. Combine onion, paprika and pepper. Rub mixture evenly over surface of brisket. Place brisket, fat side up, in large disposable aluminum pan. Add ½ cup water. Cover pan tightly with aluminum foil. Place in center of grid over very low coals. (Single layer of coals with space in between each.) Place cover on grill and cook 5 hours, turning brisket over every 1½ hours. (Remove fat from pan with baster as it accumulates.) Add ½ cup water to pan as needed. (Be sure to add briquets as needed to keep coals at very low temperature.)
(continued)

Remove foil from pan. Remove brisket; place on grid directly over very low coals. Combine pan drippings with steak sauce; reserve 1 cup for Special Sauce. Brush part of remaining steak sauce mixture over brisket. Replace cover and continue cooking 1 hour, brushing occasionally with steak sauce mixture. Serve brisket with Special Sauce.

Makes 24 to 30 servings

Special Sauce: Cook ½ cup finely chopped onion in 2 tablespoons butter until tender. Stir in 1 cup reserved steak sauce/beef drippings mixture, 1 cup ketchup, 1 tablespoon brown sugar and ¼ to ½ teaspoon crushed red pepper. Simmer 10 minutes.

Makes 2 cups

*Favorite recipe from **National Live Stock & Meat Board***

Texas-Style Deep-Dish Chili Pie

Texas-Style Deep-Dish Chili Pie

1 pound beef stew meat, cut into ½-inch cubes
1 tablespoon vegetable oil
2 cans (14½ ounces *each*) Mexican-style stewed tomatoes, undrained
1 medium green bell pepper, diced
1 package (1.25 ounces) LAWRY'S® Taco Spices & Seasonings
1 tablespoon yellow cornmeal
1 can (15¼ ounces) kidney beans, drained
1 package (15 ounces) flat refrigerated pie crusts
½ cup (2 ounces) shredded Cheddar cheese, divided

In Dutch oven, brown beef in oil; drain fat. Add stewed tomatoes, bell pepper, Taco Spices & Seasonings and cornmeal. Bring to a boil; reduce heat and simmer, uncovered, 20 minutes. Add kidney beans.

In 10-inch pie plate, unfold 1 crust and fill with chili mixture and ¼ cup cheese. Top with remaining crust, fluting edges. Bake, uncovered, in 350°F oven 30 minutes. Sprinkle remaining cheese over crust; return to oven and bake 10 minutes longer.

Makes 6 servings

Stuffed Pork Chops

4 rib pork chops, cut 1¼
    inches thick, slit for
    stuffing
1½ cups prepared stuffing
  1 tablespoon vegetable oil
    Salt and pepper
  1 bottle (12 ounces) HEINZ®
    Chili Sauce

Trim excess fat from chops. Place
stuffing in pockets of chops; secure
with wooden toothpicks or string.
In large skillet, brown chops in oil;
season with salt and pepper. Place
chops in 2-quart oblong baking
dish. Pour chili sauce over chops.

Cover with foil; bake in 350°F
oven, 30 minutes. Stir sauce; turn
and baste chops. Cover; bake an
additional 30 to 40 minutes or
until chops are cooked. Remove
toothpicks. Skim excess fat. Spoon
sauce over chops.

Makes 4 servings

**RANGE TOP COOKING
DIRECTIONS:** Stuff and brown
chops as above. Drain excess fat.
Season chops with salt and pepper;
pour chili sauce over. Cook,
covered, 30 minutes, turning chops
and basting halfway through
cooking. Remove toothpicks from
chops. Skim excess fat from sauce.

Stuffed Pork Chops

Sausage Skillet Dinner

Sausage Skillet Dinner

12 ounces fully cooked smoked
   pork link sausage, cut
   diagonally into 1-inch
   pieces
 2 tablespoons water
 1 medium onion
 2 small red apples
 2 tablespoons butter, divided
12 ounces natural frozen potato
   wedges
¼ cup cider vinegar
 3 tablespoons sugar
½ teaspoon caraway seeds
 2 tablespoons chopped fresh
   parsley

Place sausage and water in large
nonstick skillet; cover tightly and
cook over medium heat 8 minutes,
stirring occasionally. Meanwhile,
cut onion into 12 wedges; core and
cut each apple into 8 wedges.
Remove sausage to warm platter.
Pour off drippings. Cook and stir
onion and apples in 1 tablespoon
of butter in same skillet, 4 minutes
or until apples are crisp-tender.
Remove to sausage platter.

Heat remaining 1 tablespoon
butter; add potatoes and cook,
covered, over medium-high heat 5
minutes or until potatoes are
tender and golden brown, stirring
occasionally. Combine vinegar,
sugar and caraway seeds. Reduce
heat; return sausage, apple mixture
and vinegar mixture to skillet.
Cook 1 minute or until heated
through, stirring gently. Sprinkle
with parsley.   *Makes 4 servings*

*Favorite recipe from National Live
Stock & Meat Board*

Country Ham Slices with Golden Sauce

1 can (20 ounces) DOLE®
    Pineapple Slices in Juice
½ cup packed brown sugar
⅓ cup prepared yellow mustard
2 teaspoons cornstarch
¼ teaspoon ground cloves
5 slices country ham (½ inch
    thick)
2 teaspoons margarine

● Drain pineapple; reserve juice. Combine reserved juice, brown sugar, mustard, cornstarch and cloves in medium saucepan; stir until blended. Cook, stirring constantly, until sauce boils and thickens. Add pineapple. Heat through.

Country Ham Slices with Golden Sauce

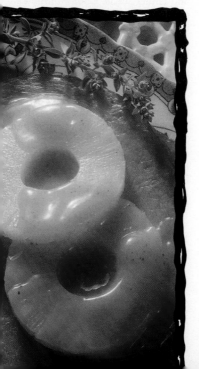

● Cook and stir ham in margarine. Serve with sauce.

Makes 5 servings

SAUCE VARIATIONS:
Asian: Add 3 tablespoons soy sauce, 1 teaspoon toasted sesame seeds.
Indian: Add 1 teaspoon curry powder.
Southwestern: Add 1 tablespoon chili powder.

Family Baked Bean Dinner

1 can (20 ounces) DOLE®
    Pineapple Chunks in Juice
½ DOLE® Green Bell Pepper,
    julienne-cut
½ cup chopped onion
1 pound Polish sausage or
    frankfurters, cut into
    1-inch chunks
⅓ cup packed brown sugar
1 teaspoon dry mustard
2 cans (16 ounces each) baked
    beans

● MICROWAVE DIRECTIONS: Drain pineapple; reserve juice for beverage. Add green pepper and onion to 13×9-inch microwavable dish.

● Cover; microwave on HIGH (100% power) 3 minutes. Add sausage, arranging around edges of dish. Cover; continue microwaving on HIGH (100% power) 6 minutes.

● In bowl, combine brown sugar and mustard; stir in beans and pineapple. Add to sausage mixture. Stir to combine. Microwave, uncovered, on HIGH (100% power) 8 to 10 minutes, stirring after 4 minutes. *Makes 6 servings*

String Pie

1 pound ground beef
½ cup chopped onion
¼ cup chopped green pepper
1 jar (15½ ounces) spaghetti
   sauce
8 ounces spaghetti, cooked
   and drained
⅓ cup grated Parmesan cheese
2 eggs, beaten
2 teaspoons butter
1 cup cottage cheese
½ cup (2 ounces) shredded
   mozzarella cheese

Cook beef, onion and green
pepper in large skillet over
medium-high heat until meat is
brown, stirring to separate meat.
Drain fat. Stir in spaghetti sauce,
mix well. Combine spaghetti,
Parmesan cheese, eggs and butter
in large bowl; mix well. Place in
bottom of 13×9-inch pan. Spread
cottage cheese over top. Pour
sauce mixture over cottage cheese.
Sprinkle mozzarella cheese over
top. Bake in preheated 350°F oven
until cheese melts, about 20
minutes.   *Makes 6 to 8 servings*

*Favorite recipe from **North Dakota Beef
Commission***

Pork Roast with Corn Bread & Oyster Stuffing

1 (5- to 7-pound) pork loin
   roast*
2 tablespoons butter or
   margarine
½ cup chopped onion
½ cup chopped celery
2 cloves garlic, minced
½ teaspoon fennel seeds,
   crushed
1 teaspoon TABASCO® pepper
   sauce
½ teaspoon salt
2 cups packaged corn bread
   stuffing mix
1 can (8 ounces) oysters,
   undrained, chopped

Preheat oven to 325°F. Make a
deep slit in back of each chop on
pork loin. In large saucepan, melt
butter; add onion, celery, garlic
and fennel seeds. Cook 5 minutes
or until vegetables are tender; stir
in TABASCO sauce and salt. Add
stuffing mix, oysters and oyster
liquid; toss to mix well.

Stuff corn bread mixture into slits
in pork. (Any leftover stuffing may
be baked in covered baking dish
during last 30 minutes of roasting.)
Place meat in shallow roasting pan.
Cook 30 to 35 minutes per pound
or until meat thermometer
inserted into meat registers 170°F.
Remove to heated serving platter.
Allow meat to stand 15 minutes
before serving.

   Makes 10 to 12 servings

* Have butcher crack backbone of
pork loin roast.

String Pie

*Butterflied Southern
Citrus Barbecue*

Butterflied Southern
Citrus Barbecue

6 to 9 pounds butterflied leg of
    lamb
1½ cups grapefruit juice
3 tablespoons brown sugar
1 tablespoon grated grapefruit
    or lemon peel
2 cloves garlic, minced
1 teaspoon ground cloves
1 teaspoon ground allspice
½ teaspoon salt
¼ teaspoon ground pepper
Few drops hot pepper sauce

Place lamb in large glass or enamel
bowl. In measuring cup, combine
remaining ingredients. Pour over
lamb. Cover and refrigerate several
hours or overnight. Drain lamb,
reserving marinade. Grill lamb 4
to 6 inches above coals or source
of heat for 1 hour and 15 minutes
or until meat thermometer
inserted in thickest part registers
140°F for rare or 150°F to 155°F
for medium. Baste with marinade.
Makes 8 servings

Favorite recipe from **American Lamb
Council, Inc.**

Mouth-Watering Roast
Pork

4 tablespoons *plus* 1½
    teaspoons unsalted butter
1 tablespoon *plus* 1½
    teaspoons pork lard or
    chicken fat (preferred) or
    vegetable oil
1 cup finely chopped onion
1 cup finely chopped celery
1 cup finely chopped green bell
    peppers
1 tablespoon *plus* 1½
    teaspoons minced garlic
2 tablespoons *plus* 1½
    teaspoons Chef Paul
    Prudhomme's PORK AND
    VEAL MAGIC®
½ teaspoon dry mustard
1 pork loin roast (4 pounds)
    (boneless or bone in)

Preheat oven to 275°F. In large
skillet, combine butter, pork lard,
onion, celery, green pepper, garlic,
Pork and Veal Magic and dry
mustard. Cook and stir about 4
minutes over high heat. Cool.

Meanwhile, place roast in baking
pan, fat side up. Make several large
slits in meat with knife, being
careful not to cut through to
bottom. (Make the slices down the
length rather than the width of the
roast so all of the carved pieces
will have some of the vegetable
mixture stuffing.) Stuff pockets
generously with vegetable mixture,
then thoroughly rub vegetable
mixture over entire roast by hand.
If any mixture is left, spread it
evenly over top and a little on
sides of roast.

Roast, uncovered, about 3 hours (or until meat thermometer inserted in meatiest part registers 160°F), then at 425°F until dark brown on top and meat is no longer pink in center, about 10 to 15 minutes. Remove from oven and let stand about 20 minutes, then slice as desired.

Makes 6 servings

Stroganoff Noodles & Meatballs

½ pound ground beef or turkey
¼ cup Italian-style dry bread
    crumbs
1 tablespoon water
1 tablespoon vegetable or olive
    oil
1½ cups water
½ cup milk
1 package LIPTON® Noodles &
    Sauce–Stroganoff
1 jar (4.5 ounces) sliced
    mushrooms, drained
1 teaspoon chopped fresh
    parsley*

In medium bowl, combine ground beef, bread crumbs and 1 tablespoon water. Shape into sixteen 1-inch meatballs. In 10-inch skillet, heat oil and cook meatballs over medium heat 5 minutes or until done; set aside.

In medium saucepan, bring 1½ cups water and milk to the boiling point. Stir in Noodles & Stroganoff Sauce and continue boiling over medium heat, stirring occasionally, 7 minutes. Stir in mushrooms, parsley and meatballs and continue cooking, stirring frequently, 3 minutes or until noodles are tender.

Makes 2 (2 cup) servings

Substitution: Use ½ teaspoon dried parsley flakes.

Stroganoff Noodles & Meatballs

Lamb & Pork Cassoulet

1 package (1 pound) dry white
    navy beans, rinsed
    Water
½ pound salt pork, sliced
1½ pounds boneless lamb
    shoulder or leg, cut into
    1-inch cubes
4 large pork chops
½ pound pork sausages
    Salt
    Pepper
2 large onions, chopped
1 can (28 ounces) tomatoes,
    drained
½ cup dry red wine
3 cloves garlic, finely chopped
¼ cup chopped fresh parsley
1 teaspoon dried thyme,
    crushed
1 bay leaf

Place beans in large bowl. Cover
with cold water; soak overnight.
Drain and rinse beans. Place beans
in Dutch oven; cover with cold
water. Bring to a boil over high
heat. Skim foam as necessary.
Reduce heat to low. Cover and
simmer about 1 hour. Drain beans,
reserving liquid.

Fry salt pork in large skillet over
medium-high heat until some of
the fat is rendered. Remove salt
pork. In batches, brown lamb, pork
chops and sausages in fat. Remove
from skillet; drain on paper towels.
Cut chops and sausages into 1-inch
pieces. Sprinkle meat with salt and
pepper. Remove all but 2
tablespoons of the fat from skillet.
Add onions. Cook and stir over
medium-high heat until onions are
tender. Add tomatoes, wine, garlic,
parsley, thyme and bay leaf.
Combine tomato mixture, drained
beans and meats in large bowl.
Spoon into large casserole. Pour
reserved bean liquid over mixture
just to cover. Bake at 350°F about
1½ hours or until meat is
fork-tender. Remove bay leaf
before serving.

Makes 6 to 8 servings

*Favorite recipe from American Lamb
Council, Inc.*

Lamb & Pork Cassoulet

Cut ham into 4 serving portions. In large skillet, cook ham in butter 3 to 4 minutes on each side or until heated through. Meanwhile, drain pineapple, reserving juice. In small bowl, combine juice, 57 Sauce, honey, mustard, cornstarch and allspice. Remove ham from skillet; keep warm. Pour 57 Sauce mixture into skillet and cook until thickened. Return ham to skillet. Top each ham portion with pineapple slice and spoon sauce over; heat through.

*Makes 4 servings
(about ⅔ cups sauce)*

Pork Chops in Raisin Sauce

2 pork chops, thick cut
1 large clove garlic, minced
    Salt and Pepper (optional)
1 teaspoon olive oil
½ teaspoon thyme, crumbled
¼ teaspoon sage
1 cup orange juice, divided
2 teaspoons cornstarch
½ cup DOLE® Raisins

● Rub pork chops with garlic. Sprinkle with salt and pepper, if desired.

● In nonstick skillet, brown chops in oil. Cover skillet during browning. Add thyme and sage; stir into pan juices.

● Mix 3 tablespoons orange juice with cornstarch. Set aside. Add remaining juice to skillet. Cover; simmer 10 minutes.

● Stir in cornstarch mixture until blended. Add raisins. Cook, stirring constantly, until sauce boils and thickens.

Makes 2 servings

Ham with Fruited Mustard Sauce

Ham with Fruited Mustard Sauce

1 fully cooked ham slice (1 to 1¼ pounds), cut ½ inch thick*
1 tablespoon butter or margarine
1 can (8 ounces) pineapple slices, undrained
¼ cup HEINZ® 57 Sauce
2 tablespoons honey
1 tablespoon prepared mustard
1½ teaspoons cornstarch
    Dash ground allspice

* A 1-pound piece of Canadian bacon, cut into 4 slices, may be substituted.

Hot & Spicy Beef Back Ribs

7 pounds beef back ribs (two
　　3½-pound slabs)
¾ cup water, divided
1 cup ketchup
2 tablespoons lemon juice
1 teaspoon ground cinnamon
1 teaspoon hot pepper sauce
½ to 1 teaspoon crushed red
　　pepper

Place each slab of ribs, meat side
down, in center of double-thick
rectangle of heavy-duty aluminum
foil. Sprinkle 2 tablespoons water
over each slab. To form packets,
bring 2 long sides of foil together
over top of ribs. Fold edges over
3 or 4 times, pressing crease in
tightly each time (allow some air
space). Flatten foil at 1 short end;
crease to form triangle and fold
edge over several times toward
package, pressing tightly to seal.
Repeat procedure on other end.
Place packets on grid directly over
low to medium coals. Place cover
on grill and cook 1½ hours,
turning packets every ½ hour.

In small saucepan, combine
ketchup, remaining ½ cup water,
lemon juice, cinnamon, hot pepper
sauce and crushed red pepper.
Bring to a boil; reduce heat and
cook 10 to 12 minutes. Remove
ribs from foil packets. Place on
grid over medium coals and grill
30 to 40 minutes, turning and
brushing with sauce occasionally.
Serve remaining sauce with ribs.

Makes about 8 servings

*Favorite recipe from **National Live
Stock & Meat Board***

Barbecued Round-Up Roast

5 pound beef round tip roast
　　or beef chuck cross rib
　　roast
1 cup strong black coffee
1 cup orange juice
1 cup chopped onion
1 tablespoon dried rosemary
1 tablespoon dried thyme
1 teaspoon ground pepper

Place roast in shallow glass baking
dish. Mix together remaining
ingredients; pour over roast. Cover;
refrigerate, turning occasionally, at
least 6 hours, no longer than 48
hours.

Prepare charcoal grill for
barbecuing. With tongs, move
glowing coals toward outside edge
of grill. Place metal drip pan in
center of grill. Push coals around
sides of drip pan. Place grill rack 6
inches above drip pan.

Cook roast on grill over
medium-hot coals, turning every
15 minutes, for 1½ to 2½ hours.
Baste occasionally with marinade
while cooking. After 1½ hours,
insert meat thermometer into
center of roast. The thermometer
should register 140°F for rare,
160°F for medium and 170°F for
well-done. Remove roast from heat
when thermometer registers 5°F
below the temperature of desired
doneness. Roast will continue to
cook after removal from heat. For
easier carving, allow roast to stand
in warm place 15 to 20 minutes.

Makes 10 to 12 servings

*Favorite recipe from **California Beef
Council***

Savory Pot Roast

1 (2½-pound) bottom round
   roast
1 tablespoon vegetable oil
½ cup A.1.® Steak Sauce
½ cup ketchup
½ cup red wine vinegar
1 teaspoon dry mustard
1 teaspoon garlic powder

In Dutch oven, over medium-high
heat, brown roast in hot oil; drain.

Blend steak sauce, ketchup,
vinegar, mustard and garlic
powder; pour over meat. Heat to a
boil; reduce heat. Cover and
simmer 2½ to 3 hours or until
meat is fork-tender, skimming and
discarding excess fat as necessary.
Slice roast and serve with pan
gravy. Garnish as desired.
Makes 6 servings

Spaghetti with Meatballs

Spaghetti with Meatballs

1½ pounds lean ground beef
1 cup finely chopped onion
¾ cup grated Parmesan cheese
½ cup fresh bread crumbs
   (1 slice)
3 cups tomato juice
4 teaspoons WYLER'S® or
   STEERO® Beef-Flavor
   Instant Bouillon
2½ teaspoons Italian seasoning
2 cloves garlic, finely chopped
8 ounces fresh mushrooms,
   sliced (about 2 cups)
1 (6-ounce) can tomato paste
1½ teaspoons sugar
1 (1-pound) package
   CREAMETTE® Spaghetti,
   cooked as package directs
   and drained

In large bowl, combine meat, ½
cup onion, cheese, crumbs, ½ *cup*
tomato juice, *2 teaspoons* bouillon
and *1¼ teaspoons* Italian
seasoning; mix well. Shape into
meatballs. In large kettle or Dutch
oven, brown meatballs; remove
from pan. In same pan, cook
remaining ½ *cup* onion, garlic and
mushrooms until tender. Stir in
remaining *2½ cups* tomato juice,
tomato paste, sugar, remaining *2
teaspoons* bouillon and *1¼
teaspoons* Italian seasoning. Add
meatballs; simmer uncovered 30 to
40 minutes. Serve with hot
spaghetti. Refrigerate leftovers.
Makes 6 to 8 servings

In large bowl, combine lamb, potatoes, green onions, peas, carrots, garlic, brown gravy and black pepper.

Place 1 sheet pie dough in pie plate; fill with lamb mixture. Cover with second sheet of pie dough. Crimp edges; cut slits in top to allow steam to escape.

Bake 30 minutes at 350°F or until pie crust is golden brown.

Makes 4 to 6 servings

*Favorite recipe from **American Lamb Council, Inc.***

Shepherd's Pie

Shepherd's Pie

- 2 cups diced cooked leg of American lamb
- 2 large potatoes, cubed and cooked
- 3 green onions, sliced
- 1 cup cooked peas
- 1 cup cooked carrot slices
- 1 clove garlic, minced
- 2 cups prepared brown gravy
- 1 teaspoon black pepper
- 2 sheets prepared pie dough*

* Or, use mashed potatoes on top in place of second crust.

Souperior Meat Loaf

- 1 envelope LIPTON® Recipe Secrets™ Onion Soup Mix
- 2 pounds ground beef
- 1½ cups fresh bread crumbs
- 2 eggs
- ¾ cup water
- ⅓ cup ketchup

Preheat oven to 350°F.

In large bowl, combine soup mix, beef, bread crumbs, eggs, water and ketchup. In 13×9-inch baking dish or roasting pan, shape into loaf. Bake 1 hour or until done. Let stand 10 minutes before serving.

Makes 8 servings

* Also terrific with LIPTON® Recipe Secrets™ Beefy Onion, Onion-Mushroom, Italian Herb with Tomato or Savory Herb with Garlic Soup Mix.

T-Bone Steaks with Vegetable Kabobs

4 beef T-bone steaks, cut 1 to
    1½ inches thick
Salt and pepper
Vegetable Kabobs (recipe
    follows)

Grill steaks over medium coals.
When first sides are browned, turn
and season with salt and pepper;
finish cooking second sides. Turn
and season. Steaks cut 1 inch
thick require about 16 minutes for
rare; 20 minutes for medium.
Steaks cut 1½ inches thick require
about 22 minutes for rare; 30
minutes for medium. Serve with
Vegetable Kabobs.

Makes 4 servings

Vegetable Kabobs
2 large potatoes (about
    1½ pounds)
1 large sweet onion
3 tablespoons butter, melted
1 teaspoon paprika
½ teaspoon celery salt
¼ teaspoon garlic powder
⅛ teaspoon freshly ground
    pepper

Cook potatoes (do not peel) in
boiling salted water 20 minutes;
drain. Cut each potato crosswise
into four 1-inch-thick slices. Cut
onion crosswise into four
1-inch-thick slices. Alternately
thread 2 potato slices and 1 onion
slice, through skin of vegetables,
on each of four 8-inch skewers.
Combine butter, paprika, celery
salt, garlic powder and pepper.
Brush both sides of vegetables
with seasoned butter. Grill kabobs
over medium coals 20 minutes,
turning after 10 minutes and
brushing with seasoned butter
occasionally.   *Makes 4 servings*

*Favorite recipe from **National Live
Stock & Meat Board***

T-Bone Steaks with Vegetable Kabobs

Patchwork Casserole

2 pounds ground beef
2 cups chopped green bell
    pepper
1 cup chopped onion
2 pounds frozen Southern-style
    hash-brown potatoes,
    thawed
2 cans (8 ounces each) tomato
    sauce
1 cup water
1 can (6 ounces) tomato paste
1 teaspoon salt
½ teaspoon dried basil,
    crumbled
¼ teaspoon ground black
    pepper
1 pound pasteurized process
    American cheese, thinly
    sliced

Preheat oven to 350°F.

Cook and stir beef in large skillet
over medium heat until crumbled
and brown, about 10 minutes;
drain off fat.

Add green pepper and onion; cook
and stir until tender, about 4
minutes. Stir in potatoes, tomato
sauce, water, tomato paste, salt,
basil and pepper.

Spoon ½ mixture into 13×9×2-
inch baking pan or 3-quart baking
dish; top with half of cheese.
Spoon remaining meat mixture
evenly on top of cheese. Cover pan
with aluminum foil. Bake 45
minutes.

Cut remaining cheese into
decorative shapes; place on top of
casserole. Let stand loosely
covered until cheese melts, about
5 minutes.

Makes 8 to 10 servings

Baked Country Cured Ham

1 country cured ham, 10 to
    14 pounds
    Whole cloves
6 cups hot water
1 cup vinegar
1 cup cider
1 tablespoon Worcestershire
    sauce
2 bay leaves
1 cup molasses

Remove rind or skin from ham
without removing the delicate layer
of fat. Gently wash ham under
running water. Pat dry and score
fat into diamond shapes. Place a
whole clove in each diamond.
Insert meat thermometer into
meaty part of ham, being careful
not to touch fat or bone. Place
ham, fat side up, in large roasting
pan with cover. Use heavy duty
alluminum foil to make a cover, if
necessary. In large bowl, combine
water, vinegar, cider and
Worcestershire sauce; pour over
ham. Place bay leaves in liquid.
Bake at 325°F 20 minutes per
pound or to an internal
temperature of 160°F. Baste often
during cooking time with molasses.
Bake uncovered last 30 minutes.
Decorate with fruit, if desired.
Cool before slicing.

Makes 20 to 25 servings

*Favorite recipe from **National Pork
Producers Council***

Patchwork Casserole

CHICKEN & TURKEY DINNERS

Dairyland Confetti Chicken

1 cup diced carrots
¾ cup chopped onion
½ cup diced celery
¼ cup chicken broth
1 can (10½ ounces) cream of chicken
    soup
1 cup dairy sour cream
3 cups cubed cooked chicken
½ cup (4 ounces) sliced mushrooms
1 teaspoon Worcestershire sauce
1 teaspoon salt
⅛ teaspoon pepper
    Confetti Topping (page 52)

(continued)

For casserole: In saucepan, combine carrots, onion, celery and chicken broth. Simmer 20 minutes. In 3-quart casserole, mix soup, sour cream, chicken cubes, mushrooms, Worcestershire sauce, salt and pepper. Add simmered vegetables and liquid; mix well. Drop tablespoons of topping onto casserole and bake in 350°F oven for 40 to 45 minutes or until golden brown. Sprinkle with remaining ¼ cup cheese and return to oven until melted. Garnish as desired.

Makes 6 to 8 servings

Confetti Topping
  1 cup sifted all-purpose flour
  2 teaspoons baking powder
  ½ teaspoon salt
  2 eggs, slightly beaten
  ½ cup milk
  1 tablespoon chopped green
      bell pepper
  1 tablespoon chopped pimiento
1¼ cups (5 ounces) shredded
      Wisconsin Cheddar cheese,
      divided

In mixing bowl, combine flour, baking powder and salt. Add eggs, milk, green pepper, pimiento and 1 cup of the cheese. Mix just until well blended.

*Favorite recipe from **Wisconsin Milk Marketing Board** ©1994*

Easy Chicken Noodle Skillet Dinner

  1 garlic clove, minced
  2 tablespoons PARKAY®
      Margarine
  2 cups quartered mushrooms
  ¼ cup dry sherry or chicken
      broth
  4 (approximately 1¼ pounds)
      boneless skinless chicken
      breasts, cut into 1-inch
      pieces
  ¾ pound VELVEETA®
      Pasteurized Process
      Cheese Spread, cubed
  1 (10-ounce) package peas,
      thawed, drained
  ¼ teaspoon pepper
  4 cups (8 ounces) wide
      noodles, cooked, drained

• Sauté garlic in margarine in large skillet. Add mushrooms and 2 tablespoons sherry. Cook 3 minutes, stirring occasionally.

• Add chicken; cook 5 to 7 minutes or until chicken is no longer pink. Reduce heat to low.

• Stir in remaining sherry, process cheese spread, peas and pepper. Cook 8 to 10 minutes or until process cheese spread is melted, stirring occasionally.

• Stir in noodles; heat thoroughly.

Makes 6 servings

Prep/Cooking time: 30 minutes

Golden Chicken Normandy-Style

Golden Chicken Normandy-Style

1 (2½ to 3 pound) chicken, cut-up
Salt and pepper
¼ cup flour
2 tablespoons butter or margarine
2 Golden Delicious apples (about 12 ounces), cored and sliced
¾ cup half-and-half
⅓ cup dry white wine
1 tablespoon lemon juice
2 tablespoons chopped fresh parsley

Season chicken with salt and pepper; coat in flour. In large skillet, melt butter. Brown chicken on all sides; remove from skillet. Add apples to skillet and brown lightly. Arrange chicken and apples in shallow 2½-quart baking dish. Bake at 350°F 20 minutes or until chicken is tender. Reserve 2 tablespoons pan drippings in skillet. Gradually add half-and-half to skillet; cook and stir until thickened. Blend in wine and lemon juice. Add salt and pepper to taste; pour over chicken and apples. Sprinkle with chopped parsley before serving.

Makes 4 servings

Favorite recipe from **Washington Apple Commission**

Chicken and Ham with Rice

¾ pound boned chicken breasts, cut into strips
4 ounces boiled ham, cut into strips
2 tablespoons butter or margarine
1 can (10¾ ounces) condensed cream of chicken soup
1 cup water
2 tablespoons Dijon-style mustard (optional)
1 package (10 ounces) asparagus cuts, thawed
1½ cups MINUTE® Rice
2 slices Swiss cheese, cut into wedges or small cubes

Chicken and Ham with Rice

● Cook and stir chicken and ham in hot butter in large skillet until lightly browned.

● Stir in soup, water and mustard; add asparagus. Bring to a boil. Stir in rice and top with cheese. Cover; remove from heat.

● Let stand 5 minutes. Fluff with fork.   *Makes 4 servings*

Homespun Turkey 'n' Vegetables

1 can (14 ounces) sliced carrots, drained
1 package (9 ounces) frozen cut green beans, thawed and drained
1 can (2.8 ounces) DURKEE® French Fried Onions, divided
1 can (16 ounces) whole potatoes, drained
1 can (10¾ ounces) condensed cream of celery soup
¼ cup milk
1 tablespoon FRENCH'S® Classic Yellow Mustard
¼ teaspoon garlic powder
1 pound uncooked turkey breast slices

Preheat oven to 375°F. In 8×12-inch baking dish, combine carrots and green beans, ½ can French Fried Onions. Slice potatoes into halves; arrange as

Homespun Turkey 'n' Vegetables

Curried Chicken Pot Pie

2 cups (10 ounces) cubed
  cooked chicken
1 bag (16 ounces) frozen
  vegetable combination
  (cauliflower, carrots,
  broccoli), thawed and
  drained
1 can (2.8 ounces) DURKEE®
  French Fried Onions
1 cup (4 ounces) shredded
  Cheddar cheese
1 can (10¾ ounces) condensed
  cream of chicken soup
⅔ cup milk
½ teaspoon seasoned salt
¼ teaspoon curry powder
1 (9-inch) folded refrigerated
  unbaked pie crust

Preheat oven to 400°F. In 9-inch
pie plate, combine chicken,
vegetables, ½ can French Fried
Onions and ½ cup cheese. In small
bowl, combine soup, milk,
seasoned salt and curry powder;
pour over chicken mixture and stir
to combine. Place pie crust over
chicken mixture; seal edges and
cut 4 steam vents. Bake,
uncovered, at 400°F for 40
minutes or until crust is golden
brown. Top with remaining cheese
and onions; bake, uncovered, 2 to
3 minutes or until onions are
golden.   *Makes 4 to 6 servings*

many halves as will fit, cut-side
down around edges of baking dish.
Combine any remaining potatoes
with vegetables in dish. In medium
bowl, combine soup, milk, mustard
and garlic powder; pour half of the
soup mixture over vegetables.
Overlap turkey slices on
vegetables. Pour remaining soup
mixture over turkey and potatoes.
Bake, covered, at 375°F for 40
minutes or until turkey is done.
Top turkey with remaining onions;
bake, uncovered, 3 minutes or
until onions are golden.

Makes 4 servings

Grilled Roaster with International Basting Sauces

1 PERDUE® Oven Stuffer
    Roaster (5 to 7 pounds)
    Salt
    Ground pepper
1 cup vegetable oil
⅓ cup red wine vinegar
1 teaspoon paprika

Remove and discard giblets from roaster; rinse bird and pat dry with paper towels. Sprinkle inside and out with salt and pepper; set aside. To prepare basting sauce, in small covered jar, combine oil, vinegar, paprika, 1 teaspoon salt and ½ teaspoon pepper. Shake well; set aside.

If using a gas grill, follow manufacturer's directions. If using a covered charcoal grill, prepare coals at least 30 minutes before grilling. Open all vents and place a drip pan at center in bottom of grill. Arrange 25 to 30 hot coals at either end of drip pan. For added smoky flavor, soak 1 cup mesquite, hickory, oak, apple or cherry wood chips in water and scatter onto hot coals.

When coals are covered with gray ash and are medium-hot (you can hold your hand over them 3 to 4 seconds), place roaster on grill over drip pan. Cover with grill lid and cook roaster about 2 hours until Bird Watcher thermometer pops up and juices run clear with no hint of pink when thigh is pierced. (Note: Smoking may cause meat to remain slightly pink.) Begin checking roaster for doneness after 1½ hours. If thermometer has popped, brush on basting sauce and grill 30 minutes longer. In small saucepan, bring remaining basting sauce to a boil; serve with carved roaster. Do not reuse sauce.

Makes 6 servings

SAUCE VARIATIONS:

Italian Roaster: Prepare basting sauce as directed above, adding 2 cloves minced garlic, 1 cup ketchup, 1 teaspoon dried oregano and ½ teaspoon dried basil to mixture. Use only in last 10 minutes grilling.

French Roaster: Prepare basting sauce as directed above, adding ⅓ cup minced shallots, ⅓ cup Dijon-style mustard and 1 teaspoon crumbled dried tarragon to mixture.

German Roaster: Prepare basting sauce as directed above, adding ½ cup beer, 2 tablespoons molasses and 2 tablespoons caraway seeds to mixture. Use only in last 10 minutes grilling.

Chinese Roaster: Prepare basting sauce as directed above, adding ⅓ cup soy sauce, 2 cloves minced garlic and 1 teaspoon ground ginger or 1 tablespoon grated fresh ginger root to mixture.

*Grilled Roaster
with International
Basting Sauces*

Turkey Cottage Pie

¼ cup butter or margarine
¼ cup all-purpose flour
1 envelope LIPTON® Recipe Secrets™ Golden Onion Soup Mix
2 cups water
2 cups cut-up cooked turkey or chicken
1 package (10 ounces) frozen mixed vegetables, thawed
1¼ cups shredded Swiss cheese (about 5 ounces), divided
⅛ teaspoon pepper
5 cups hot mashed potatoes

Preheat oven to 375°F.

In large saucepan, melt butter and cook flour, stirring constantly, 5 minutes or until golden. Stir in golden onion soup mix thoroughly blended with water. Bring to a boil, then simmer 15 minutes or until thickened. Stir in turkey, vegetables, 1 cup cheese and pepper. Turn into lightly greased 2-quart casserole; top with hot potatoes, then remaining ¼ cup cheese. Bake 30 minutes or until bubbling.

Makes about 8 servings

MICROWAVE DIRECTIONS: In 2-quart casserole, heat butter at HIGH (100% power) 1 minute. Stir in flour and heat uncovered, stirring frequently, 2 minutes. Stir in golden onion soup mix thoroughly blended with water. Heat uncovered, stirring occasionally, 4 minutes or until thickened. Stir in turkey, vegetables, 1 cup cheese and pepper. Top with hot potatoes, then remaining ¼ cup cheese. Heat uncovered, turning casserole occasionally, 5 minutes or until bubbling. Let stand uncovered 5 minutes. For additional color, sprinkle, if desired, with paprika.

Turkey Cottage Pie

Down-Home Corn and Chicken Casserole

2 chickens (2 to 3 pounds *each*), each cut into 10 pieces
3 tablespoons Chef Paul Prodhomme's POULTRY MAGIC®, in all
⅓ cup vegetable oil
8 cups fresh corn, cut off cob (about twelve 8-inch ears), in all
3½ cups finely chopped onions
1½ cups finely chopped green bell peppers
1 pound tomatoes, peeled, chopped
3½ cups water
2 cups uncooked rice

Remove excess fat from chickens; season chicken pieces with 2 tablespoons of the Poultry Magic and place in plastic bag. Seal and refrigerate overnight.

Heat oil in an 8-quart roasting pan over high heat until it just starts to smoke, about 6 minutes. Add the 10 largest pieces of chicken (skin side down first) and brown, cooking 5 minutes on each side. Remove chicken and reheat oil about 1 minute or until oil stops sizzling. Brown remaining chicken 5 minutes on each side. Remove and keep warm.

Add half of corn to hot oil. Scrape bottom of pan well to get up all browned chicken bits and stir to mix well. Let corn cook, without stirring, about 6 minutes. You want it to brown and to start breaking down starch. Add ½ tablespoon Poultry Magic and stir to combine. Let mixture cook, without stirring, about 7 minutes to continue

Down-Home Corn and Chicken Casserole

browning process. Stir in onions, bell peppers and remaining ½ tablespoon Poultry Magic. Cover with tight-fitting lid and cook about 5 minutes. Add remaining corn and tomatoes. Stir to mix well; cover and cook 10 minutes. Transfer corn mixture to another pan and keep warm. Preheat oven to 400°F.

Add water and rice to roasting pan. Bring to a boil, stirring occasionally. Layer chicken pieces on top of rice and cover chicken layer with corn mixture. Cover and bake 25 minutes.

Remove casserole from oven. Let stand 10 minutes, covered, and then serve.   *Makes 8 servings*

Creamy Turkey & Broccoli

1 package (6 ounces) stuffing
 mix,* *plus* ingredients to
 prepare mix
1 can (2.8 ounces) DURKEE®
 French Fried Onions
1 package (10 ounces) frozen
 broccoli spears, thawed
 and drained
1 package (1⅛ ounces) cheese
 sauce mix
1¼ cups milk
 ½ cup sour cream
 2 cups (10 ounces) cubed
 cooked turkey or chicken

Preheat oven to 350°F. In medium
saucepan, prepare stuffing mix
according to package directions;
stir in ½ can French Fried Onions.
Spread stuffing over bottom of
greased 9-inch round baking dish.
Arrange broccoli spears over
stuffing with florets around edge of
dish. In medium saucepan, prepare
cheese sauce mix according to
package directions using 1¼ cups
milk. Remove from heat; stir in
sour cream and turkey. Pour
turkey mixture over broccoli
stalks. Bake, covered, at 350°F for
30 minutes or until heated
through. Sprinkle remaining
onions over turkey; bake,
uncovered, 5 minutes or until
onions are golden.

Makes 4 to 6 servings

* Three cups leftover stuffing may
be substituted for stuffing mix. If
stuffing is dry, stir in water, 1
tablespoon at a time, until moist
but not wet.

Creamy Turkey & Broccoli

Chili Tomato Grilled Chicken

2 tablespoons cooking oil
½ cup finely chopped onion
1 clove garlic, minced
1 chicken bouillon cube
½ cup hot water
1 can (8 ounces) taco sauce or tomato sauce
1 teaspoon salt
¼ teaspoon dried oregano leaves
2 tablespoons vinegar
1 tablespoon prepared mustard
4 to 6 broiler-fryer chicken quarters
1 tablespoon mild chili powder

In small skillet, heat oil to medium temperature. Add onion and garlic; cook and stir about 3 minutes or until onion is tender. Dissolve bouillon cube in hot water; add bouillon, taco sauce, salt, oregano, vinegar and mustard to skillet. Dip chicken into sauce mixture, then lightly sprinkle chili powder on all sides of quarters. Add remaining chili powder to sauce; bring to a boil and remove from heat.

Just before grilling, dip each chicken quarter in sauce again. Cook on charcoal grill 45 to 60 minutes or until chicken can easily be pierced with fork (the white meat will be done before the dark). Turn every 10 minutes during grilling, basting with sauce during last half of grilling time.   *Makes 4 to 6 servings*

*Favorite recipe from **National Broiler Council***

Chili Tomato Grilled Chicken

No-Peek Skillet Chicken

2 tablespoons olive or vegetable oil
2½-to 3-pound chicken, cut into serving pieces
1 can (14½ ounces) whole peeled tomatoes, undrained
1 jar (4½ ounces) sliced mushrooms, drained
1 clove garlic, minced
1 envelope LIPTON® Recipe Secrets™ Onion Soup Mix
Hot cooked noodles
Chopped fresh parsley

In 12-inch skillet, heat oil and brown chicken; drain. Stir in tomatoes, mushrooms and garlic combined with soup mix. Simmer, covered, 45 minutes or until chicken is tender. Serve, if desired, with hot noodles and chopped fresh parsley.
            Makes about 6 servings

Chicken Skillet Supper

1½ teaspoons salt
¼ teaspoon pepper
¼ teaspoon ground paprika
⅛ teaspoon garlic powder
1 broiler-fryer chicken (about 3 pounds), cut into serving pieces
1 tablespoon vegetable oil
2 tablespoons water
1 medium onion, chopped
1 medium potato, peeled, cut into 2¼-inch strips
1 tablespoon slivered almonds (optional)
1 can (8 ounces) tomato sauce
1 cup chicken broth
1 teaspoon sugar
1 package (10 ounces) frozen French-cut green beans or mixed vegetables

Mix salt, pepper, paprika and garlic powder in small bowl; rub over chicken. Heat oil in large skillet over medium heat; add chicken, skin-side down. Cover and cook 10 minutes. Add water to chicken; cover and cook 30 minutes longer, turning chicken over every 10 minutes. Remove chicken from skillet; reserve.

Add onion, potato and almonds to drippings in skillet; cook until onion is tender, about 3 minutes. Add tomato sauce, broth and sugar to onion mixture; cook until liquid comes to a boil. Add beans and chicken pieces to tomato mixture; cover and cook until beans are tender, about 10 minutes. Serve hot.   *Makes 4 to 6 servings*

Tasty Turkey Roll

1 pound ground turkey
½ cup soft bread crumbs
¼ cup tomato juice
1 egg, beaten
2 cloves garlic, minced
¼ teaspoon dried oregano
¼ teaspoon pepper
¼ pound shaved turkey ham
1 cup grated mozzarella cheese
2 tablespoons chili sauce (optional)

In medium bowl, combine ground turkey, bread crumbs, juice, egg, garlic, oregano and pepper.

On rectangular 16×12-inch piece of waxed paper, shape turkey mixture into 12×9-inch rectangle. Place turkey ham over top of turkey mixture and sprinkle cheese over turkey ham. Roll turkey, jelly-roll style, using waxed paper to help make roll. Lightly press ends of roll to seal. Place turkey roll, seam side down on baking sheet, lightly coated with nonstick cooking spray.

Bake at 350°F 1 hour or until center of turkey roll reaches 160°F on meat thermometer and ground turkey is no longer pink.

To serve, drizzle 2 tablespoons chili sauce over top of roll, if desired, and cut into 12 equal pieces.   *Makes 12 servings*

*Favorite recipe from **National Turkey Federation***

Chicken Skillet Supper

Old-Fashioned Chicken With Dumplings

3 to 3½ pounds chicken pieces
3 tablespoons butter or
   margarine
2 cans (14½ ounces *each*)
   ready-to-serve chicken
   broth
3½ cups water
1 teaspoon salt
¼ teaspoon white pepper
2 large carrots, cut into 1-inch
   slices
2 ribs celery, cut into 1-inch
   slices
8 to 10 small boiling onions
¼ pound small mushrooms, cut
   into halves
   Parsley Dumplings (recipe
   follows)
½ cup frozen peas, thawed,
   drained

Brown chicken in melted butter in
6- to 8-quart saucepan over
medium-high heat. Add broth,
water, salt and pepper. Bring to a
boil over high heat. Reduce heat to
low. Cover; simmer 15 minutes.
Add carrots, celery, onions and
mushrooms. Simmer, covered, 40
minutes or until chicken and
vegetables are tender. Prepare
Parsley Dumplings.

When chicken is tender, skim fat
from broth. Stir in peas. Drop
dumpling mixture into broth,
making 6 large or 12 small
dumplings. Cover; simmer 15 to 20
minutes or until dumplings are
firm to the touch and wooden pick
inserted in center comes out
clean.　　　*Makes 6 servings*

Parsley Dumplings: Sift 2 cups
all-purpose flour, 4 teaspoons
baking powder and ½ teaspoon
salt into medium bowl. Cut in 5
tablespoons cold butter or
margarine until mixture resembles
coarse meal. Make a well in center;
pour in 1 cup milk, all at once.
Add 2 tablespoons chopped
parsley; stir with fork until dough
cleans side of bowl.
　　　Makes 6 large or
　　　12 small dumplings.

Chicken, Sausage 'n' Shrimp Gumbo

1 can (28 ounces) whole
   tomatoes, undrained
3 chicken breast halves,
   boned, skinned and cut
   into 1½-inch pieces
½ pound Creole or smoked
   Polish sausage, sliced
   ½ inch thick
2 bay leaves
1 teaspoon freshly ground
   black pepper
1 teaspoon thyme
⅛ to ¼ teaspoon cayenne
   pepper or to taste
2 cups chicken broth
1 cup UNCLE BEN'S®
   CONVERTED® Brand Rice
¾ cup coarsely chopped onion
¾ cup sliced celery
2 large garlic cloves, crushed
¼ cup water
3 tablespoons flour
1 pound medium shrimp,
   peeled and deveined
1 large green pepper, cut into
   ¾-inch squares
¼ cup minced parsley

Coarsely chop tomatoes, reserving juice. Combine tomatoes, juice, chicken, sausage, bay leaves, black pepper, thyme and cayenne pepper in large skillet. Bring to a boil. Reduce heat. Cover and simmer 15 minutes. Meanwhile, bring chicken broth to a boil in medium saucepan. Stir in rice, onion, celery and garlic. Cover tightly and simmer 20 minutes. Blend water with flour until smooth. Add to skillet with shrimp and green pepper. Cook, uncovered, stirring occasionally, until shrimp are cooked through and gumbo is thickened, 5 to 7 minutes. Remove rice from heat. Let stand covered until all liquid is absorbed, about 5 minutes. Stir in parsley. Remove bay leaves. Divide gumbo evenly between 6 large shallow soup plates. Top each serving with rice. *Makes 6 servings*

Potluck Pockets

Nonstick cooking spray
½ pound lean ground turkey
¾ cup chopped onions
1 clove garlic, minced
½ cup sliced mushrooms
1 jar (14 ounces) spaghetti sauce
2½ cups all-purpose flour, divided
½ cup cornmeal
2 teaspoons baking powder
½ teaspoon dried oregano leaves
¼ cup margarine
1¼ cups KELLOGG'S® ALL-BRAN® cereal
1 cup skim milk
½ cup (2 ounces) shredded part-skim mozzarella cheese

In large skillet coated with nonstick cooking spray, cook turkey, onions and garlic over medium heat. Stir in mushrooms and spaghetti sauce. Cover; simmer an additional 20 minutes, stirring occasionally.

In medium bowl, stir together 2 cups flour, cornmeal, baking powder and oregano. With pastry blender, cut in margarine until mixture resembles coarse crumbs.

In small bowl, combine Kellogg's® All-Bran® cereal and milk. Let stand 3 minutes or until milk is absorbed. Add cereal mixture to flour mixture, stirring with fork until dough forms ball.

On lightly floured surface, knead in remaining flour until dough is smooth and elastic. Divide dough in half; roll to ⅛-inch thickness. With pastry cutter or small saucepan lid cut dough into 6-inch rounds. Cover each round with 2 teaspoons cheese; top with ¼ cup turkey mixture. Fold rounds in half, pinching dough with fork to seal. Repeat with remaining dough. Place on baking sheet coated with nonstick cooking spray.

Bake at 350°F 20 minutes or until lightly browned. Serve warm.
Makes 12 servings

Bacon and Creamy Herb Noodles

1 package (12 ounces) LOUIS RICH® Turkey Bacon, cut into ½-inch pieces
8 ounces fresh mushrooms, sliced
6 green onions with tops, sliced
8 ounces uncooked medium egg noodles
1 package (8 ounces) Neufchâtel or light cream cheese, cubed
⅓ cup *each* white wine and water *or* ⅔ cup skim milk
½ teaspoon *each* garlic powder, dried basil and dried thyme leaves
1 small tomato, chopped

Heat Turkey Bacon in nonstick skillet over medium heat about 10 minutes or until lightly browned, stirring frequently. Add mushrooms and onions; cook and stir an additional 4 minutes. Reserve. Meanwhile, cook noodles according to package directions in large saucepan or Dutch oven; drain. Return noodles to saucepan; add remaining ingredients except tomato. Cook and stir over medium heat until cheese melts and sauce is well blended. Add reserved Turkey Bacon mixture; toss to combine. Sprinkle with tomato before serving. Garnish as desired. *Makes 8 servings*

Spicy Chicken Cacciatore

¼ cup flour
1 teaspoon salt
½ teaspoon freshly ground black pepper
2 pounds chicken breasts and thighs, skinned
2 tablespoons olive oil
¾ cup PACE® Picante Sauce
1 can (8 ounces) tomato sauce
¼ cup dry red wine
8 ounces mushrooms, halved or quartered, as desired
2 cloves garlic, minced
1 teaspoon dried basil leaves, crushed
1 teaspoon dried oregano leaves, crushed
1 small green bell pepper, cut into short, thin strips

In medium bowl, combine flour, salt and pepper. Coat chicken in flour mixture. Cook chicken in oil in large, deep skillet or Dutch oven until lightly browned on both sides, about 8 minutes; drain. Add picante sauce, tomato sauce, red wine, mushrooms, garlic, basil and oregano to skillet. Cover and simmer 20 minutes. Stir in pepper strips; simmer, uncovered, about 10 minutes or until chicken is tender and sauce has thickened. Serve with additional Pace® Picante Sauce. *Makes 6 servings*

asty Turkey Pot Pie

Tasty Turkey Pot Pie

½ cup MIRACLE WHIP® Salad
    Dressing
2 tablespoons flour
1 teaspoon instant chicken
    bouillon
⅛ teaspoon pepper
¾ cup milk
½ cups chopped cooked turkey
    or chicken
1 (10-ounce) package frozen
    mixed vegetables, thawed,
    drained
1 (4-ounce) can refrigerated
    crescent rolls

• Combine salad dressing, flour,
bouillon and pepper in medium
saucepan. Gradually add milk.

• Cook, stirring constantly, over
low heat until thickened. Add
turkey and vegetables; heat
thoroughly, stirring occasionally.

• Spoon into 8-inch square baking
dish. Unroll dough into two
rectangles. Press perforations
together to seal. Place rectangles
side-by-side to form square; press
edges together to form seam.
Cover turkey mixture with dough.

• Bake at 375°F 15 to 20 minutes
or until browned.
Makes 4 to 6 servings

Preparation time: 15 minutes
Baking time: 20 minutes

Variations: Combine 1 egg,
beaten, and 1 tablespoon cold
water, mixing until well blended.
Brush dough with egg mixture just
before baking.

Substitute one chicken bouillon
cube for instant chicken bouillon.

Substitute 10×6-inch baking dish
for 8-inch square baking dish.

Substitute 12×8-inch baking dish
for 8-inch square dish.

Double all ingredients. Assemble
recipe as directed, using three
dough rectangles to form top
crust. Decorate crust with cut-outs
from remaining rectangle. Bake as
directed.

SPECIALTIES OF THE SEA

Chesapeake Crab Strata

4 tablespoons butter or margarine
4 cups unseasoned croutons
2 cups shredded Cheddar cheese
2 cups milk
8 eggs, beaten
½ teaspoon dry mustard
½ teaspoon seafood seasoning
  Salt and black pepper to taste
1 pound crabmeat, picked over to remove
  any shell

Preheat oven to 325°F. Place butter in
11×7×1½-inch baking dish. Heat in oven until
melted, tilting to coat dish. Remove dish from
oven; spread croutons over melted butter. Top
with cheese; set aside.

Combine milk, eggs, dry mustard, seafood
seasoning, salt and black pepper; mix well.
Pour egg mixture over cheese in dish and
sprinkle crabmeat on top. Bake for 50 minutes
or until mixture is set. Remove from oven and
let stand for about 10 minutes. Garnish with
pepper rings.

Makes 6 to 8 servings

Scandinavian Salmon-Cheddar Pie

- 3 large eggs
- ¼ cup milk
- 3 tablespoons chopped parsley, divided
- 2 tablespoons butter, melted
- 2 tablespoons minced green onion
- 1 tablespoon *plus* 1 teaspoon lemon juice
- 1 teaspoon Worcestershire sauce
- ½ teaspoon dry mustard
- 2 cups (8 ounces) shredded Wisconsin Cheddar cheese
- ½ pound fresh cooked, flaked salmon *or* 1 can (6½ ounces) salmon, drained, deboned and flaked
- 1 (9-inch) pie shell, baked and cooled
- ¾ cup dairy sour cream
- ¼ cup finely chopped cucumber
- 1 teaspoon dill weed
- ⅛ teaspoon ground white pepper

Heat oven to 425°F. Beat eggs in large bowl; add milk, 2 tablespoons parsley, butter, green onion, 1 tablespoon lemon juice, Worcestershire sauce and mustard; mix well. Fold in cheese and salmon; pour into cooled pie shell. Bake 20 to 25 minutes or until just set and crust is golden brown. Let stand 10 minutes before serving. Combine sour cream, cucumber, remaining 1 tablespoon parsley, dill, remaining 1 teaspoon lemon juice and pepper; mix well. Dollop each serving with sour cream mixture.   *Makes 6 servings*

Favorite recipe from Wisconsin Milk Marketing Board ©1994

Scandinavian Salmon-Cheddar Pie

Salmon Linguini Supper

Salmon Linguini Supper

8 ounces linguini, cooked in
   unsalted water and
   drained
1 package (10 ounces) frozen
   peas
1 cup milk
1 can (10¾ ounces) condensed
   cream of celery soup
¼ cup (1 ounce) grated
   Parmesan cheese
⅛ teaspoon tarragon, crumbled
   (optional)
1 can (15½ ounces) salmon,
   drained and flaked
1 egg, slightly beaten
¼ teaspoon salt
¼ teaspoon ground black
   pepper
1 can (2.8 ounces) DURKEE®
   French Fried Onions,
   divided

Preheat oven to 375°F. Return hot
pasta to saucepan; stir in peas,
milk, soup, cheese and tarragon;
spoon into 8×12-inch baking dish.
In medium bowl, using fork,
combine salmon, egg, salt, pepper
and ½ can French Fried Onions.
Shape salmon mixture into 4 oval
patties. Place patties on pasta
mixture. Bake, covered, at 375°F
40 minutes or until patties are
done. Top patties with remaining
onions; bake, uncovered, 3
minutes or until onions are golden
brown.   *Makes 4 servings*

MICROWAVE DIRECTIONS:
Prepare pasta mixture as above,
except increase milk to 1¼ cups;
spoon into 8×12-inch
microwavable dish. Cook, covered,
at HIGH (100% power) 3 minutes;
stir. Prepare salmon patties as
above using 2 eggs. Place patties
on pasta mixture. Cook, covered,
at HIGH (100% power) 10 to 12
minutes or until patties are done.
Rotate dish halfway through
cooking time. Top patties with
remaining onions; cook,
uncovered, at HIGH (100% power)
1 minute. Let stand 5 minutes.

Shrimp in Angel Hair Pasta Casserole

1 tablespoon butter
2 eggs
1 cup half-and-half
1 cup plain yogurt
½ cup (4 ounces) shredded
    Swiss cheese
⅓ cup crumbled feta cheese
⅓ cup chopped fresh parsley
¼ cup chopped fresh basil *or*
    1 teaspoon dried basil
    leaves, crushed
1 teaspoon dried oregano
    leaves, crushed
1 package (9 ounces)
    uncooked fresh angel hair
    pasta
1 jar (16 ounces) mild, thick
    and chunky salsa
1 pound medium shrimp,
    peeled and deveined
½ cup (4 ounces) shredded
    Monterey Jack cheese
Snow peas (optional)
Plum tomatoes stuffed with
    cottage cheese (optional)

With 1 tablespoon butter, grease 12×8-inch pan. Combine eggs, half-and-half, yogurt, Swiss cheese, feta cheese, parsley, basil and oregano in medium bowl; mix well. Spread ½ the pasta on bottom of prepared pan. Cover with salsa. Add ½ the shrimp. Cover with remaining pasta. Spread egg mixture over pasta and top with remaining shrimp. Sprinkle Monterey Jack cheese over top. Bake in preheated 350°F oven 30 minutes or until bubbly. Let stand 10 minutes. Garnish with snow peas and stuffed plum tomatoes, if desired.   *Makes 6 servings*

*Favorite recipe from **Southeast United Dairy Industry Association, Inc.***

Herb-Baked Fish & Rice

1½ cups hot chicken bouillon
½ cup uncooked regular rice
¼ teaspoon Italian seasoning
¼ teaspoon garlic powder
1 package (10 ounces) frozen
    chopped broccoli, thawed
    and drained
1 can (2.8 ounces) DURKEE®
    French Fried Onions
1 tablespoon grated Parmesan
    cheese
1 pound unbreaded fish fillets
    (thawed if frozen)
Paprika
½ cup (2 ounces) shredded
    Cheddar cheese

Preheat oven to 375°F. In 8×12-inch baking dish, combine hot bouillon, uncooked rice and seasonings. Bake, covered, at 375°F for 10 minutes. Top with broccoli, ½ can French Fried Onions and Parmesan cheese. Place fish fillets diagonally down center of dish; sprinkle fish lightly with paprika. Bake, covered, at 375°F 20 to 25 minutes or until fish flakes easily with fork. Stir rice. Top fish with Cheddar cheese and remaining onions; bake, uncovered, 3 minutes or until onions are golden.
          Makes 3 to 4 servings

Shrimp in Angel Hair Pasta Casserole

Baked Fish with Potatoes and Onions

Baked Fish with Potatoes and Onions

1 pound baking potatoes, very
 thinly sliced
1 large onion, very thinly
 sliced
1 small red or green bell
 pepper, thinly sliced
 Salt
 Black pepper
½ teaspoon dried oregano
 leaves, crushed, divided
1 pound lean fish fillets, cut
 1 inch thick
¼ cup butter or margarine
¼ cup all-purpose flour
2 cups milk
¾ cup (3 ounces) shredded
 Cheddar cheese

Preheat oven to 375°F.

Arrange ½ potatoes in buttered
3-quart casserole. Top with ½
onion and ½ bell pepper. Season
with salt and black pepper.
Sprinkle with ¼ teaspoon oregano.
Arrange fish in 1 layer over
vegetables. Arrange remaining
potatoes, onion and bell pepper
over fish. Season with salt, black
pepper and remaining ¼ teaspoon
oregano; set aside.

Melt butter in medium saucepan
over medium heat. Stir in flour;
cook until bubbly, stirring
constantly. Gradually stir in milk.
Cook until thickened, stirring
constantly. Pour white sauce over
casserole. Cover and bake at 375°F
40 minutes or until potatoes are
tender. Sprinkle with cheese.
Bake, uncovered, about 5 minutes
more or until cheese is melted.

Makes 4 servings

Company Crab

1 pound blue crabmeat, fresh,
  frozen or pasteurized
1 can (15 ounces) artichoke
  hearts, drained
1 can (4 ounces) sliced
  mushrooms, drained
2 tablespoons butter or
  margarine
2½ tablespoons all-purpose flour
½ teaspoon salt
⅛ teaspoon ground red pepper
1 cup half-and-half
2 tablespoons dry sherry
2 tablespoons crushed corn
  flakes
1 tablespoon grated Parmesan
  cheese
  Paprika

Thaw crabmeat if frozen. Remove
any pieces of shell or cartilage.
Cut artichoke hearts in half. Place
artichokes in well-greased, shallow
1½-quart casserole. Add crabmeat
and mushrooms; cover and set
aside.

Melt butter over medium heat in
small saucepan. Stir in flour, salt
and ground red pepper. Gradually
stir in half-and-half. Continue
cooking until sauce thickens,
stirring constantly. Stir in sherry.
Pour sauce over crabmeat.
Combine crumbs and cheese in
small bowl; sprinkle over
casserole. Sprinkle with paprika.
Bake in preheated 450°F oven 12
to 15 minutes or until bubbly.
                    Makes 6 servings

*Favorite recipe from **Florida Bureau of
Seafood and Aquaculture***

Quick and Easy Tuna Rice with Peas

1 package (10 ounces) green
  peas
1¼ cups water
1 can (11 ounces) condensed
  cheddar cheese soup
1 can (12½ ounces) tuna,
  drained and flaked
1 chicken bouillon cube
1½ cups MINUTE® Rice

● Bring peas, water, soup, tuna and
bouillon cube to a full boil in
medium saucepan. Stir in rice.
Cover; remove from heat. Let
stand 5 minutes. Fluff with
fork.   *Makes 4 servings*

*Quick and Easy Tuna Rice
with Peas*

Farm-Raised Catfish with Bacon and Horseradish

6 (4- to 5-ounce) farm-raised catfish fillets, fresh or frozen
2 tablespoons butter
¼ cup chopped onion
1 (8-ounce) package cream cheese, softened
¼ cup dry white wine
2 tablespoons shredded horseradish
1 tablespoon Dijon-style mustard
½ teaspoon salt
⅛ teaspoon pepper
4 strips bacon, cooked crisp, crumbled
2 tablespoons finely chopped fresh parsley, for garnish

If frozen, thaw fish fillets according to package directions; rinse and pat dry. Preheat oven to 350°F. Grease large baking dish. Arrange fillets in single layer in dish.

Melt butter in small skillet over medium-high heat. Add onion; cook and stir until softened. Combine cream cheese, wine, horseradish, mustard, salt and pepper in small bowl; stir in onion. Pour this mixture over fish and top with crumbled bacon. Bake 30 minutes or until fish flakes easily when tested with fork. Garnish with parsley. Serve immediately.

Makes 6 servings

Seafood Pasta Salad

1 can (15¼ ounces) DOLE® Tropical Fruit Salad
6 ounces spiral pasta, cooked
2 teaspoons toasted sesame oil
Fruity Dressing (recipe follows)
12 ounces cooked baby shrimp
2 cups (4 ounces) bean sprouts
1 cup snow peas
½ cup chopped DOLE® Celery
½ cup chopped DOLE® Red Bell Pepper
¼ cup DOLE® Chopped Dates
¼ cup dry roasted peanuts, coarsely chopped

• Drain tropical fruit salad; reserve ⅓ cup juice for dressing.

• Toss hot pasta with sesame oil. When cool, mix with Fruity Dressing.

• Add tropical fruit salad and remaining ingredients; toss to combine. *Makes 8 servings*

Fruity Dressing
¼ cup rice or white vinegar
2 tablespoons light soy sauce
2 tablespoons chopped fresh cilantro or parsley
1 teaspoon minced jalapēno or serrano chile

• Combine ⅓ cup juice, reserved from Tropical Fruit Salad, vinegar, soy sauce, cilantro and jalapēno; whisk to blend.

Farm-Raised Catfish with Bacon and Horseradish

OLD-FASHIONED DESSERTS

Peanut Chocolate Surprise Pie

8 tablespoons (1 stick) butter, melted
1 cup granulated sugar
2 eggs
½ cup all-purpose flour
½ cup chopped peanuts
½ cup chopped walnuts
½ cup semisweet chocolate chips
¼ cup bourbon
1 teaspoon vanilla extract
1 (9-inch) unbaked deep-dish pie shell
Whipped cream, for garnish
Chocolate shavings, for garnish

Preheat oven to 350°F. Cream butter and sugar in large bowl. Add eggs and beat until well mixed. Gradually add flour, then stir in nuts, chips, bourbon and vanilla. Spread mixture evenly in unbaked pie shell. Bake 40 minutes. Cool pie on wire rack; decorate with whipped cream and chocolate shavings.

Makes one 9-inch pie

Golden Apple Pie with Rum Sauce

Preheat oven to 425°F. Roll out remaining pastry to 10-inch circle; cut into ¾-inch strips. Arrange strips in lattice pattern on top of apples and trim at edges; pinch edges of bottom and top crust together and flute edge of pie, if desired.

Bake 20 minutes. *Reduce oven temperature to 375°F.* Bake 35 to 40 minutes or until apples are tender. If necessary, loosely cover top of pie with foil to prevent overbrowning. Meanwhile, prepare Rum Sauce. To serve, cool pie at least 20 minutes; cut into slices and spoon Rum Sauce over each slice.   *Makes 10 servings*

Rum Sauce: In medium saucepan, combine 1 cup sugar, ¾ cup water, and ½ teaspoon ground cinnamon. Bring to boil over medium-high heat; boil 5 minutes, stirring occasionally. Remove from heat. In small bowl, blend 2 tablespoons cornstarch and ¼ cup cold water; gradually stir into hot sugar mixture. Return to heat and cook, stirring constantly, until mixture bubbles and thickens. Stir in ¼ cup rum. Serve sauce warm.

Favorite recipe from Washington Apple Commission

Golden Apple Pie with Rum Sauce

Pastry for 2-crust 9-inch pie
6 to 7 Golden Delicious apples
¼ cup firmly packed brown sugar
2 tablespoons all-purpose flour
½ teaspoon ground cinnamon
¼ teaspoon ground nutmeg
¼ teaspoon salt (optional)
¼ cup chopped nuts
Rum Sauce (recipe follows)

Line 9-inch pie plate with half of pastry; reserve remaining pastry. Peel, core and slice apples to equal 7 cups. In large bowl, combine apples, sugar, flour, cinnamon, nutmeg and salt. Transfer apple mixture to pastry-lined plate.

California Apricot-Cherry Cornmeal Cobbler

2 cups sliced fresh California apricots (about 1 pound)
⅓ cup granulated sugar
2 cups pitted fresh California cherries (about 8 ounces)
1 tablespoon all-purpose flour

BISCUIT DOUGH

1 cup all-purpose flour
½ cup yellow cornmeal
½ tablespoons *plus* 1 teaspoon granulated sugar
2 teaspoons baking powder
¼ teaspoon salt
½ teaspoon grated orange peel
5 tablespoons unsalted butter, chilled
¾ cup low fat milk

Preheat oven to 375°F. In small bowl, combine apricots and ⅓ cup sugar. In separate bowl, combine cherries and 1 tablespoon flour; set both aside. For Biscuit Dough, in large bowl, combine flour, cornmeal, 1½ tablespoons sugar, baking powder and salt; add orange peel. Cut in butter until mixture resembles coarse meal. Add milk; combine just until dry ingredients are moistened. Combine fruit in 1½-quart baking dish; spoon batter over top. Sprinkle with remaining 1 teaspoon sugar. Bake 25 to 30 minutes or until golden brown. Cool slightly and serve.

Makes 8 servings

Favorite recipe from **California Apricot Advisory Board**

California Apricot-Cherry Cornmeal Cobbler

Orange Ambrosia Cake Roll

CAKE

- 1 cup cake flour
- 1 teaspoon baking powder
- ¼ teaspoon salt
- 3 eggs
- 1 cup sugar
- ⅓ cup fresh squeezed orange juice
- Grated peel of ½ SUNKIST® Orange
- Orange slices (optional)
- Maraschino cherries (optional)

ORANGE FILLING AND GLAZE

- ¾ cup sugar
- 1 tablespoon cornstarch
- 1 cup fresh squeezed orange juice
- 4 egg yolks, beaten
- 1 cup heavy cream or whipping cream, whipped
- Grated peel of 1 SUNKIST® Orange
- ¼ cup shredded or flaked coconut

Line 15½×10½×1-inch jelly roll pan with greased aluminum foil. In medium bowl, combine cake flour, baking powder and salt. In large bowl, with electric mixer, beat eggs well. Gradually add sugar and orange juice, beating until well blended. Gradually add dry ingredients, beating just until smooth. Stir in orange peel. Pour batter into prepared pan. Bake at 375°F 13 to 15 minutes. Cool 5 minutes. Invert cake onto large, waxed paper-lined cookie sheet; carefully remove foil. Roll up cake with waxed paper starting at narrow end; cool completely on wire rack.

To make Orange Filling and Glaze, in saucepan, combine sugar and cornstarch. Gradually blend in orange juice and beaten egg yolks. Bring to a boil over medium heat, stirring until thickened. Cool thoroughly. Reserve ½ cup cooled filling for glaze. Gently fold whipped cream and orange peel into remaining 1 cup filling.

To assemble cake roll, unroll cake and spread with filling. Reroll without waxed paper and place on serving platter. Spread top with reserved glaze and sprinkle with coconut. Chill for at least 1 hour before serving. Garnish with orange twists and well-drained maraschino cherries with stems, if desired.

Makes 8 to 12 servings

Karen Ann's Lemon Cake

CAKE

- 2 cups all-purpose flour
- 1½ teaspoons baking powder
- ½ teaspoon baking soda
- ¼ teaspoon salt
- ⅔ cup butter or margarine, softened
- 1¼ cups granulated sugar
- 3 eggs, separated
- ¾ cup sour cream
- Grated peel of 1 SUNKIST® Lemon
- Lemony Frosting (page 83)

Line two 8-inch round cake pans with waxed paper. Preheat oven to 350°F. In medium bowl, combine flour, baking powder, baking soda and salt. In large bowl, with electric mixer, cream together butter and sugar. Beat in egg yolks one at a time; continue beating until light in color. Add dry ingredients to creamed mixture alternately with sour cream, beating just until smooth. With clean beaters, beat egg whites until soft peaks form. Gently fold beaten egg whites and lemon peel into batter. Pour batter into prepared pans. Bake at 350°F for 30 to 35 minutes or until wooden pick inserted in center comes out clean. Cool 10 minutes. Remove from pans and peel off waxed paper. Cool on wire racks. Fill and frost with Lemony Frosting.

Makes 12 servings

Lemony Frosting

½ cup butter or margarine, softened
3 cups confectioners' sugar, divided
Grated peel of ½ SUNKIST® Lemon
2 tablespoons fresh squeezed lemon juice

In medium bowl, cream together butter and 1 cup confectioners' sugar. Add lemon peel, lemon juice and remaining 2 cups sugar; beat until smooth.

Makes about 1¾ cups frosting

Left to right: Orange Ambrosia Cake Roll; Karen Ann's Lemon Cake

Apricot-Pear Strudel

2 sheets frozen puff pastry
1 (17-ounce) can California
   apricots, drained and
   sliced
1 (16-ounce) can pears,
   drained and cut into
   chunks
½ cup blanched slivered
   almonds
¼ cup packed light brown
   sugar
½ teaspoon ground cinnamon
½ teaspoon nutmeg
1 egg, beaten with 1 teaspoon
   water

Thaw pastry 20 minutes; unfold
and place second sheet directly on
top of first sheet. Roll on lightly
floured surface to 14×10-inch
rectangle. In large bowl, combine
apricots, pears, almonds, brown
sugar, cinnamon and nutmeg.
Spoon fruit filling lengthwise down
center third of pastry. Brush edges
with egg-water mixture. Fold left
side of pastry over filling; fold right
side of pastry over to enclose
filling completely. Pinch edges to
seal. Roll strudel over onto
ungreased baking sheet; seal edges
by pressing with fork. Brush top
with egg-water mixture; refrigerate,
covered, 30 minutes or overnight.
Preheat oven to 425°F. With sharp
knife, lightly score top of strudel.
Bake 25 to 30 minutes or until
puffed and golden brown. Cool on
wire rack for 30 minutes.

Makes 8 servings

Favorite recipe from **California Apricot
Advisory Board**

Brown Sugar Pumpkin Pie

⅓ cup FLEISCHMANN'S®
   Margarine
1¼ cups all-purpose flour
4 to 5 tablespoons cold water
¾ cup EGG BEATERS® 99%
   Egg Product
1 (16-ounce) can solid-pack
   pumpkin
½ cup skim milk
½ cup firmly packed dark
   brown sugar
½ teaspoon ground allspice
½ teaspoon ground cinnamon
½ teaspoon ground ginger

In medium bowl, cut margarine
into flour until mixture is crumbly;
stir in enough water until mixture
forms a ball. Set aside ¼ of the
dough; roll remaining dough into
an 11-inch circle, about ⅛ inch
thick. Place in 9-inch pie plate;
trim edge even with pie plate. Roll
out reserved dough and cut into
1-inch leaves; make vein markings
in each leaf with back of knife.
Attach leaves to edge of crust
using 1 tablespoon egg product.
Chill crust until ready to fill.

In medium bowl, blend remaining
egg product, pumpkin, skim milk,
brown sugar, allspice, cinnamon
and ginger. Pour into prepared
crust. Bake at 375°F for 45 to
50 minutes or until set. Cool
completely on wire rack.

Makes 8 servings

Apricot-Pear Strudel

Berry Cobbler

1 pint fresh raspberries
  (2½ cups)*
1 pint fresh blueberries or
  strawberries, sliced
  (2½ cups)*
⅓ cup sugar
2 tablespoons cornstarch
1 cup all-purpose flour
1 tablespoon sugar
1½ teaspoons baking powder
¼ teaspoon salt
½ cup milk
⅓ cup butter or margarine,
  melted
¼ teaspoon ground nutmeg

Berry Cobbler

Preheat oven to 375°F. Combine berries, ⅓ cup sugar and cornstarch in medium bowl; toss lightly to coat. Spoon into 1½-quart or 8-inch square baking dish. Combine flour, 1 tablespoon sugar, baking powder and salt in medium bowl. Add milk and butter; mix just until dry ingredients are moistened. Drop six heaping tablespoonfuls of batter evenly over berries; sprinkle with nutmeg. Bake 25 minutes or until topping is golden brown and fruit is bubbly. Cool on wire rack. Serve warm or at room temperature.

Makes 6 servings

*One (16-ounce) bag frozen raspberries and one (16-ounce) bag frozen blueberries or strawberries may be substituted for fresh berries. Thaw berries, reserving juices. Increase cornstarch to 3 tablespoons.

Pickled Peaches

6 pounds firm-ripe peaches,
  peeled, pitted and halved
6¾ cups sugar
3½ cups white vinegar (labeled
  5% acidity)
4 (2½-inch) cinnamon sticks
1 tablespoon whole cloves
1 tablespoon ground ginger

Combine sugar and vinegar in a 6- to 8-quart saucepan. Bring to a boil for 5 minutes. Tie spices in spice bag or cheesecloth. Add spice bag and peaches to syrup. Simmer 5 to 10 minutes or until peaches are cooked but not too soft, stirring peaches gently to cook all sides. Cover and let stand

n cool place for 12 to 18 hours,
tirring peaches 2 or 3 times.
Bring peaches and syrup to a boil.
Remove from heat and remove
pices. Skim off foam, if necessary.
mmediately fill hot pint or quart
ars with mixture, leaving ½-inch
eadspace.

Carefully run nonmetallic utensil
own inside of jars to remove
rapped air bubbles. Wipe jar tops
nd threads clean. Place hot lids
n jars and screw bands on firmly.
rocess in Boiling Water Canner
page 29) 25 minutes for quarts or
0 minutes for pints.

*Makes about 2 quarts
or 4 to 5 pints*

*Old-Fashioned
Upside-Down Cake*

Old-Fashioned
Upside-Down Cake

⅔ cup margarine, divided
⅔ cup brown sugar, packed
1 can (20 ounces) DOLE®
      Pineapple Slices in Syrup
      or Juice
10 maraschino cherries
¾ cup granulated sugar,
      divided
2 eggs, separated
1 teaspoon grated lemon peel
1 teaspoon lemon juice
1 teaspoon vanilla extract
½ cups all-purpose flour
¾ teaspoons baking powder
¼ teaspoon salt
½ cup dairy sour cream

Melt ⅓ cup margarine in 10-inch
ast iron skillet. Remove from
eat. Add brown sugar and stir
ntil blended.

Drain pineapple well; reserve
tablespoons syrup. Arrange
ineapple in sugar mixture. Place
erry in center of each slice.

• Beat remaining ⅓ cup margarine
with ½ cup granulated sugar until
light and fluffy. Beat in egg yolks,
lemon peel, lemon juice and
vanilla.

• Combine flour, baking powder
and salt. Blend into creamed
mixture alternately with sour
cream and reserved 2 tablespoons
pineapple syrup.

• Beat egg whites to soft peaks.
Gradually beat in remaining ¼ cup
granulated sugar until stiff peaks
form. Fold into batter. Pour over
pineapple in skillet. Bake in 350°F
oven about 35 minutes or until
wooden pick inserted in center
comes out clean. Let stand 10
minutes, then invert onto serving
plate. Serve warm or cold.

Makes 8 servings

Apple-Buttermilk Pie

2 medium-size Granny Smith
  apples
3 eggs
1½ cups sugar, divided
1 cup buttermilk
⅓ cup margarine or butter,
  melted
2 tablespoons all-purpose flour
2 teaspoons vanilla extract
1 tablespoon ground
  cinnamon, divided
2 teaspoons ground nutmeg,
  divided
1 (9-inch) unbaked pie shell

Preheat oven to 350°F. Peel and
core apples; cut into small chunks.
Place apples in bowl; cover with
cold water and set aside. Beat eggs
briefly at low speed of electric
mixer until mixed. Add all but
1 teaspoon sugar, buttermilk,
margarine, flour, vanilla, 2
teaspoons cinnamon and 1½
teaspoons nutmeg; mix at low
speed until well blended. Drain
apples thoroughly and place in
unbaked pie shell. Pour buttermilk
mixture over apples. Combine
remaining 1 teaspoon sugar,
1 teaspoon cinnamon and ½
teaspoon nutmeg; sprinkle over
top. Bake 50 to 60 minutes. Serve
warm or at room temperature for
the best flavor. Store in
refrigerator.

Makes one 9-inch pie

Apple-Buttermilk Pie

Gingerbread Cookies

½ cup FLEISCHMANN'S®
    Margarine, softened
¾ cup firmly packed light
    brown sugar
¾ cup light molasses
¼ cup EGG BEATERS® 99%
    Egg Product
½ cups all-purpose flour
2 teaspoons baking soda
2 teaspoons ground cinnamon
2 teaspoons ground ginger
½ teaspoon ground cloves
½ teaspoon ground nutmeg
    Frosting and assorted
    candies for decorating

ream margarine and sugar. Beat
molasses and egg product.
mbine flour, baking soda and
ices. Stir into margarine mixture
make stiff dough. Divide dough
half; wrap and chill for several
urs or overnight.

ll small amount of dough out
to well greased and floured
king sheets. Cut with desired
nch cookie cutters. Remove
aps and reroll. Bake at 350°F
8 to 10 minutes or just until set
d lightly brown. Cool completely
wire racks. Decorate cookies
h frosting and assorted candies.

Makes 4 dozen cookies

Shimmering Pineapple Gelatin

Shimmering Pineapple Gelatin

1 can (20 ounces) DOLE®
    Pineapple Slices in Juice
1 package (3 ounces) gelatin,
    any flavor
1 cup boiling water

- Drain juice from can of
pineapple, leaving slices in can.

- Dissolve gelatin in boiling water.

- Fill can of pineapple with
dissolved gelatin. Refrigerate until
set. Refrigerate extra gelatin in a
bowl.

- To unmold, run hot water on can
sides and bottom to loosen. Open
other end of can and use end to
push mold out.

- Cut between pineapple slices.
With a fork, break up chilled
gelatin in bowl. Spoon onto serving
plates with pineapple slices.

Makes 5 servings

Fresh Lemon Meringue Pie

In large saucepan, combine sugar, cornstarch and salt. Gradually blend in cold water and lemon juice. Stir in egg yolks. Add butter and boiling water. Bring to a boil over medium-high heat, stirring constantly. Reduce heat to medium and boil 1 minute. Remove from heat; stir in lemon peel and food coloring. Pour into baked pie crust. Top with Three-Egg Meringue, sealing well at edges. Bake at 350°F 12 to 15 minutes. Cool 2 hours before serving.   *Makes 6 serving*

Three-Egg Meringue
   3 egg whites
   ¼ teaspoon cream of tartar
   6 tablespoons sugar

In large bowl, with electric mixer, beat egg whites with cream of tartar until foamy. Gradually add sugar and beat until stiff peaks form.

Fresh Lemon Meringue Pie

1½ cups sugar
   ¼ cup *plus* 2 tablespoons
      cornstarch
   ½ teaspoon salt
   ½ cup cold water
   ½ cup fresh squeezed lemon
      juice
   3 egg yolks, well beaten
   2 tablespoons butter or
      margarine
1½ cups boiling water
      Grated peel of ½ SUNKIST®
      Lemon
   2 to 3 drops yellow food
      coloring (optional)
   1 (9-inch) baked pie crust
      Three-Egg Meringue (recipe
      follows)

Rocky Road Banana Pudding

   1 package (4-serving size)
      chocolate pudding and pi◄
      filling mix (not instant)
   2 cups low fat milk
   2 DOLE® Bananas, peeled,
      sliced
   2 cups miniature
      marshmallows
   ½ cup chopped walnuts

● Combine pudding mix and milk in saucepan. Prepare pudding according to package directions. Cool.

● Fold bananas, marshmallows an◄ nuts into cooled pudding.
                  Makes 6 servin◄

Baked Apple Donuts

3 cups unsifted all-purpose
   flour
¾ cups sugar, divided
½ teaspoons baking powder
½ teaspoon salt
½ teaspoon grated orange peel
¼ teaspoon ground nutmeg
¾ cups butter or margarine
1 cup grated Golden Delicious
   apple, peeled, cored and
   coarsely chopped
1 cup vanilla-flavored yogurt
2 large eggs, beaten
1 teaspoon ground cinnamon

Heat oven to 350°F. Grease 24
muffin cups or line muffin cups
with paper liners. In large bowl,
combine flour, 1 cup sugar, baking
powder, salt, orange peel and
nutmeg. With pastry blender or
two knives, cut in ¾ cup (1½
sticks) butter until mixture
resembles coarse meal.

In medium bowl, combine apple,
yogurt and eggs; add to flour
mixture stirring until just
combined. Spoon batter into
prepared muffin cups; bake 20 to
25 minutes or until centers spring
back when gently pressed.
Meanwhile, melt remaining ½ cup
(1 stick) butter and combine
remaining ¾ cup sugar with
cinnamon.

Cool donuts in pan 5 minutes.
Remove from pan and cool until
able to handle; roll tops of donuts
in melted butter then
cinnamon-sugar mixture and
serve.   *Makes 24 donuts*

Favorite recipe from **Washington Apple
Commission**

Baked Apple Donuts

ACKNOWLEDGMENTS

The publishers would like to thank the companies and organizations listed below for the use of their recipes in this publication.

American Lamb Council
Armour Swift-Eckrich
Borden Kitchens, Borden, Inc.
California Apricot Advisory Board
California Beef Council
Canned Food Information Council
Chef Paul Prudhomme's Magic
Seasoning Blends
Dole Food Company, Inc.
Florida Department of Citrus
Heinz U.S.A.
The HVR Company
Kellogg Company
Kerr Group Inc.
Kraft General Foods, Inc.
Lawry's Foods, Inc.
Thomas J. Lipton Co.
Louis Rich Company

McIlhenny Company
Nabisco Foods Group
National Broiler Council
National Live Stock & Meat Board
National Pork Producers Council
National Turkey Federation
North Dakota Beef Commission
North Dakota Wheat Commission
Pace Foods, Inc.
Perdue Farms
Reckitt & Colman Inc.
Sargento Cheese Company, Inc.
Southeast United Dairy Industry
Association, Inc.
Sunkist Growers, Inc.
Uncle Ben's Rice
Washington Apple Commission
Wisconsin Milk Marketing Board

PHOTO CREDITS

The publishers would like to thank the companies and organizations listed below for the use of their photographs in this publication.

American Lamb Council
Borden Kitchens, Borden, Inc.
California Apricot Advisory Board
Chef Paul Prudhomme's Magic
Seasoning Blends
Dole Food Company, Inc.
Heinz U.S.A.
The HVR Company
Kraft General Foods, Inc.
Lawry's Foods, Inc.

Thomas J. Lipton Co.
National Broiler Council
National Live Stock & Meat Board
Pace Foods, Inc.
Perdue Farms
Reckitt & Colman Inc.
Sargento Cheese Company, Inc.
Sunkist Growers, Inc.
Washington Apple Commission
Wisconsin Milk Marketing Board

INDEX

METRIC CONVERSION CHART

VOLUME MEASUREMENTS (dry)

⅛ teaspoon = 0.5 mL

¼ teaspoon = 1 mL

½ teaspoon = 2 mL

¾ teaspoon = 4 mL

1 teaspoon = 5 mL

1 tablespoon = 15 mL

2 tablespoons = 30 mL

¼ cup = 60 mL

⅓ cup = 75 mL

½ cup = 125 mL

⅔ cup = 150 mL

¼ cup = 175 mL

1 cup = 250 mL

2 cups = 1 pint = 500 mL

3 cups = 750 mL

4 cups = 1 quart = 1 L

VOLUME MEASUREMENTS (fluid)

1 fluid ounce (2 tablespoons) = 30 mL

4 fluid ounces (½ cup) = 125 mL

8 fluid ounces (1 cup) = 250 mL

12 fluid ounces (1½ cups) = 375 mL

16 fluid ounces (2 cups) = 500 mL

WEIGHTS (mass)

½ ounce = 15 g

1 ounce = 30 g

3 ounces = 90 g

4 ounces = 120 g

8 ounces = 225 g

10 ounces = 285 g

12 ounces = 360 g

16 ounces = 1 pound = 450 g

DIMENSIONS

1/16 inch = 2 mm

⅛ inch = 3 mm

¼ inch = 6 mm

½ inch = 1.5 cm

¾ inch = 2 cm

1 inch = 2.5 cm

OVEN TEMPERATURE

250°F = 120°C

275°F = 140°C

300°F = 150°C

325°F = 160°C

350°F = 180°C

375°F = 190°C

400°F = 200°C

425°F = 220°C

450°F = 230°C

BAKING PAN SIZES

Utensil	Size in Inches/ Quarts	Metric Volume	Size in Centimeters
Baking or Cake Pan (square or rectangular)	8×8×2	2 L	20×20×
	9×9×2	2.5 L	22×22×
	12×8×2	3 L	30×20×
	13×9×2	3.5 L	33×23×
Loaf Pan	8×4×3	1.5 L	20×10×
	9×5×3	2 L	23×13×
Round Layer Cake Pan	8×1½	1.2 L	20×4
	9×1½	1.5 L	23×4
Pie Plate	8×1¼	750 mL	20×3
	9×1¼	1 L	23×3
Baking Dish or Casserole	1 quart	1 L	—
	1½ quart	1.5 L	—
	2 quart	2 L	—